BIGGEST JOKE BOOK
in the World
· · · · ·

BIGGEST JOKE BOOK
in the World

• • • • •

Matt Rissinger & Philip Yates

Illustrated by Jeff Sinclair

Sterling Publishing Co., Inc.
New York

Library of Congress Cataloging-in-Publication Data

Rissinger, Matt.
    Biggest joke book in the world / by Matt Rissinger and Philip
Yates ; illustrated by Jeff Sinclair.
            p.   cm.
    Includes index.
    ISBN 0-8069-0852-1
    1. Wit and humor, Juvenile.   [1. Jokes.]   I. Yates, Philip,
1956–   .   II. Sinclair, Jeff, ill.   III. Title.
PN6163.R55   1995
818'.5402—dc20   94-45605
                                                                      CIP
                                                                       AC

10   9   8   7   6   5   4   3   2   1

First paperback edition published in 1996 by
Sterling Publishing Company, Inc.
387 Park Avenue South, New York, N.Y. 10016
© 1995 by Matt Rissinger & Philip Yates
Distributed in Canada by Sterling Publishing
℅ Canadian Manda Group, One Atlantic Avenue, Suite 105
Toronto, Ontario, Canada M6K 3E7
Distributed in Great Britain and Europe by Cassell PLC
Wellington House, 125 Strand, London WC2R 0BB, England
Distributed in Australia by Capricorn Link (Australia) Pty Ltd.
P.O. Box 6651, Baulkham Hills, Business Centre, NSW 2153, Australia
Manufactured in the United States of America
All rights reserved

Sterling ISBN 0-8069-0852-1 Trade
                   0-8069-0853-X Paper

To Mom: Don't worry, I haven't quit my day job yet. —M.R.

To Maria Beach: There's love in every moonbeam. You're right, they were bullfrogs. —P.Y.

Contents

1. Quick Takes

MIKE: My sister's on a banana diet.
SPIKE: Has she lost weight?
MIKE: No, but you should see her climb trees.

TRUDY: How do you like my hair?
JUDY: Did you set it?
TRUDY: Yes, I did.
JUDY: When does it go off?

MISSY: Do you like my hair?
CHRISSY: Yes, but why don't you keep it on a leash where it belongs?

> "Doctor, what can you give me
> for my kleptomania?"
> "How about Klepto-Bismol?"

PATIENT: I keep having this dream that I'm a boat crashing into a dock. What should I do?
DOCTOR: Sounds like you need pier (peer) counseling.

DOCTOR: I don't like the look of your husband.
WIFE: Neither do I, but he's great with the kids.

TEENSY: Sometimes I can't stand you.
WEENSY: You don't sit so well with me, either.

CUSTOMER: Excuse me, do you have any loafers?
SHOE SALESMAN: As a matter of fact, we do.
CUSTOMER: Well, could you get one to wait on me?

BARBER: Your hair needs cutting badly.
CUSTOMER: No, it needs cutting nicely. You cut it badly last time.

WAITRESS: Have I kept you waiting long?

CUSTOMER: No, but did you know that there are 3,479 rose patterns on your wallpaper?

TIM: When I open my own pet shop, you can visit me and all the dumb animals.

JIM: Be sure and wear your glasses so I'll know which one is you.

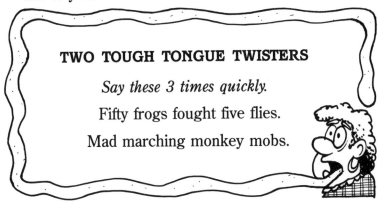

TWO TOUGH TONGUE TWISTERS

Say these 3 times quickly.

Fifty frogs fought five flies.

Mad marching monkey mobs.

BEN: One Christmas Eve Santa Claus decided to give his reindeer a vacation. In their place, he got eight monkeys to pull the sleigh. The names of the monkeys were Do, Re, Fa, So, La, Ti and Do.

LEN: Hey, what about Mi?

BEN: All right, you can pull the sleigh, too.

"Excuse me, waiter, but does your chef have chicken legs?"

"I don't know—I can't see under his apron."

IGGY: Hey, Ziggy, why are you so sad?

ZIGGY: My sister said she wouldn't talk to me for 30 days.

IGGY: Why should that make you sad?

ZIGGY: Today's her last day.

SISTER: You're not very smart!
BROTHER: Don't I go to school, stupid?
SISTER: Yes, and you come home the same way!

COMPUTER SALES CLERK: This little computer will do half your work for you.
COMPUTER CUSTOMER: In that case, I'll take two.

He's so dumb, he trips over the cordless phone.

"Why have you cut a big hole in your umbrella?"
"So I can see when it stops raining."

LENNY: What's a sassafras?
DENNY: Something you shouldn't do to a 900-pound fras.

CUSTOMER: Waitress, how long have you been working here?
WAITRESS: About two months.
CUSTOMER: Oh, then it couldn't have been you who took my order.

CUSTOMER: Waiter, how do you serve shrimps here?
WAITER: On bended knee.

CUSTOMER: Waiter, what is this fly doing in my hamburger?
WAITER: Looks like the cha-cha-cha.

My dog is so dumb, he chases bones and buries cars.

"Doctor, will you give me something for my head?"
"Thanks, but I have enough heads as it is."

IKE: Is it all right if I crash at your place tonight?
SPIKE: Sure, but don't expect me to pull you from the wreckage.

FATHER: Son, what kind of marks do you expect to get in gym class?
SON: No marks, Dad, just a lot of bruises.

UNCLE ERNIE: How about a little folding money for your birthday?
BERNIE: Gee, are you going to bend a quarter in half like you did last year?

Knock-knock.
  Who's there?
Weirdo.
  Weirdo who?
Weirdo the deer and the
  antelopes play?

Knock-knock.
  Who's there?
Cash.
  Cash who?
No, thanks, I prefer
pistachios.

MANDY: Where do spies do their shopping?
CANDY: At the snooper market.

PALEONTOLOGIST #1: Why were some dinosaurs big,
  green and scaly?
PALEONTOLOGIST #2: Because if they were small, fuzzy,
  and yellow, they'd have been tennis balls.

JERRY: It rained the whole week I was on vacation.
TERRY: Looks like you got a good tan.
JERRY: That isn't tan, it's rust.

REX: Just how stupid do you think I am?
DEX: Somewhere between a pet rock and a pet gerbil.

MOLLY: Would you say I'm a person of rare
  intelligence?
DOLLY: Yes. it's rare when you show any.

NICKY: Go ahead and pick my brain, if you want.
RICKY: I don't think I have a pair of tweezers small
  enough.

  "You have the brain of an idiot."
  "Want it back?"

MUFFY: If tires hold up cars, what holds up an
  airplane?
DUFFY: Hijackers.

MAUD: Sometimes I get so depressed I want to drown
  myself.
CLAUDE: What stops you?
MAUD: I can't swim.

Wise Man Says

He who laughs last didn't
get the joke.

Too many beauticians
mousse things up.

JOE: What's the difference between a fisherman and a dunce?

MOE: I give up.

JOE: A fisherman baits its hook and a dunce hates his book.

DANA: I think I can put this wallpaper on myself.

LANA: Well, go ahead, but I think it would look better on the wall.

MORRIS: Why are you moving out of your house?

BORIS: According to statistics, more accidents happen at home.

TIP: What is yellow, sweet and extremely dangerous?

TOP: Shark-infested apple sauce.

HUSBAND: Hey, honey, look at the new VCR I got.

WIFE: You know we can't afford a VCR.

HUSBAND: Don't worry, I traded the TV for it.

STORE CLERK: Are you interested in a color TV, sir?

CUSTOMER: Yes, but I'm not sure what color to get.

DELLA: Where would you find a homeless octopus?
STELLA: On squid (skid) row.

Did you hear about the goofy weatherman who took a ruler outside to see how long it was going to rain?

Knock-knock.
    Who's there?
Nod.
    Nod who?
Nod you again!

LYNN: What is huge, green, lives in a swamp, and is very scary?
MIN: A five-ton frog.

ED: How do you tell the difference between an iguana, a crybaby and the Roadrunner?
RED: That's easy. One creeps, one weeps and one beeps.

Parachute Recall Notice: On page 8 of instruction manual, please change the words "state zip code" to "pull rip cord."

Policemen listen to criminal records.

LONI: How can I improve my mind?
RONNY: Read a blank book.

TEACHER: Stop acting like an idiot!
SEYMOUR: Who's acting?

PAT: I broke a mirror so I'm supposed to get seven years' bad luck.
KAT: Don't worry, I know a lawyer who can get you five.

MACK: What did the lonely fog say to the lonely beach?
JACK: I mist (missed) you.

NITA: What do you call a little bear that never bathes?
RITA: Winnie-the-Phew!

2. Kid Crack-Ups

"Hello, may I speak to Jimmy?"

"I'm sorry, Jimmy's only a baby. He hasn't learned to talk yet."

"That's okay, I'll wait."

Suzie's mother sent her to the store to buy diapers for the new baby. "That'll be eight dollars for the diapers," said the clerk, "and thirty cents for the tax."

"Oh, we don't use tacks," said Suzie. "When my mother changes the baby, she just fastens them with pins."

JENNIE: Why were you born in a taxi cab?
BENNIE: I wanted to be near my mother.

JILL: Why were you born on Mount Everest?
BILL: I wanted to reach my peak at an early age.

Mrs. Smith and Mrs. Jones were discussing their children's sleeping habits. "I have trouble getting Wilbur up in the morning," said Mrs. Smith.

"It's never a problem for me," replied Mrs. Jones. "When it's time for him to get up, I toss the cat into his bed."

"How does that get him up?"

"Because," said Mrs. Jones, "he sleeps with the dog."

RYAN: My cat is a mindreader.
BRIAN: Where did you find her?
RYAN: At the ESP-CA.

MILLIE: My parents left me an only child.
WILLIE: What did you do?
MILLIE: What could I do? I raised him like he was my brother.

WHEN I GROW UP . . .

CINDY: When I grow up, I want to be a deep-sea diver.
MINDY: Isn't that a little out of your depth?

SKIP: When I grow up, I want to be a dentist.
FLIP: Isn't that going to take a lot of pull?

HOLEY: When I grow up, I want to be a chiropractor.
MOLEY: Be prepared for a lot of back talk.

SHARI: When I grow up, I want to be a ballet dancer.
BARRY: That'll keep you on your toes!

FLORRIE: My new baby sister is cute as a button.
MORRIE: What's so cute about her?
FLORRIE: She has a round head with four holes in the middle.

JOE: My sister has a sun complex.
MOE: What's that?
JOE: She thinks that everything revolves around her.

CLINT: My sister's in the hospital with spotted fever.
FLINT: Is it serious?
CLINT: No, they spotted it just in time.

Johnny got separated from his father at Disney World and soon found himself in the hands of a security guard.

"What's your father like?" asked the guard.

"Fast cars and football," came the boy's reply.

STAN: Yesterday I climbed a ladder, fell 30 feet and survived without a scratch.

FRAN: How did you manage that?

STAN: It was in the swimming pool.

Little Willy showed off his singing parrot to his friend Rickie.

"If you pull his left leg," said Willy, "he'll sing 'God Bless the Queen.' Pull his right leg and he'll sing 'The Star-Spangled Banner.'"

"What happens if you pull both legs?" asked Rickie.

"Squawk!" said the parrot. "I fall off the perch, you idiot!"

SIGN AT BABY DIAPER SERVICE

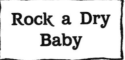

Rock a Dry Baby

Little Sara found a jigsaw puzzle and worked on it every night for two weeks until it was finished. "Look what I did!" she said, showing off the puzzle to her best friend.

"Wow, how long did it take you?" asked her friend.

"Two weeks—can you believe it?"

"You call that fast?" said her friend, unimpressed.

"You bet it is," replied Sara, showing her friend the puzzle box. "Look—it says 'From Two to Four Years.'"

DINKY: I've had such a terrible day! First I was shot, then I was blown up, then I was framed and hung!

INKY: I know. I hate to have my picture taken too.

A kindly old woman watched as a little boy tried to reach the doorbell of the house next door. Deciding she would help, the woman walked over and rang the bell for him.

"Well, what now?" said the woman to the boy.

"Run like crazy," said the boy, "That's what I'm going to do!"

Knock-knock.
    Who's there?
Pasta.
    Pasta who?
    Pasta your bedtime, isn't it?

Fax machines can be dangerous. I know a kid who got his shirtsleeve caught in one and two minutes later he was in Australia.

JACK: Knock-knock.
JILL: Who's there?
JACK: Eiffel.
JILL: Eiffel who?
JACK: Eiffel down and broke my crown.

DALE: A member of my family thinks he's a pen.
GALE: And who might that be?
DALE: My Bic brother.

An old man was sitting in a plane next to a six-year-old boy who had never been in a plane before. "They say," smiled the old man, as they prepared for takeoff, "that when you look out the window of an airplane, people look like ants."

"It's true!" said the boy. "Look, there's my Aunt Millie and there's my Aunt Betty..."

When little Joey came home from school with another black eye, his mother scolded him. "Have you been fighting again?"

"Sorry, Mom."

"I thought I told you the next time you need to control your temper to count to ten."

"I did," said Joey. "But Billy's mother only told him to count to five, so he punched me first!"

LETTERS FROM CAMP

from Chess camp:
Dear Mother: The days are okay but having trouble with the knights.

from Diet camp:
Dear Mother and Dad: Building a birdhouse out of popsicle sticks. Please send 500 popsicles.

from Rocket camp:
Dear Dad: Everybody here is getting fired up.

The two boys were camping in the backyard. When they couldn't figure out what time it was, the first boy said to the second, "Start singing very loud."

"How will that help?" said the second boy.

"Just do it," insisted the first.

Both boys broke into song, singing at the top of their lungs. Moments later, a neighbor threw open her window and shouted, "Keep it down! Don't you know it's three o'clock in the morning?"

3. Grin or Lose!

RANDY: My dad quit smoking cold turkey.

SANDY: How does he feel?

RANDY: Better, but he's still coughing up the feathers.

BOY *(to zoo attendant):* I'd like three tickets. One for me and two for my sister.

ZOO ATTENDANT: Why do you want two tickets for your sister?

BOY: One to get her in and one to get her out.

Two men, fishing in stormy weather, suddenly found themselves in rough water, surrounded by ferocious sharks. As the sharks argued over which got the pick of the two, a lawyer shark swam over and offered some counsel.

"I'll help settle this matter," said the lawyer to the two fishermen. "But it's going to cost you an arm and a leg."

The Amazon was full of hostile cannibals, but that didn't stop Chet and Miles from camping deep in the jungle. In the middle of the night they were suddenly awakened by the sound of drums. PUM-pum-pum-pum! PUM-pum-pum-pum!

As the beats got closer and closer, Chet said to Miles, "I don't like the sound of those drums."

Just then, one of the cannibals stepped out of the bush and said, "Yeah, well, that's not our regular drummer."

HOW DO I GET TO . . . ?

How do I get to the cemetery from here?
Make a dead right.

How do I get to the Crossword Company?
Go three blocks down and five across.

How do I get to the army base from here?
Go three blocks and make a left, right, left, right, left . . ."

MEL: I feel like an old bed.
BELLE: Why, because everybody keeps turning you down?

Did you hear about the absent-minded professor who drove his stove to the store? He was arrested for riding the range.

MAY I SPEAK TO . . . ?

"May I speak to the butcher?"
"Sorry, he's in a meating."

"May I speak to the Invisible Man?"
"Sorry, I haven't seen him around."

"May I speak to the person in charge of gift wrap?"
"Sorry, she's all tied up."

"Do you sell ladders?"
"Sorry, rung number."

Two tortoises were walking down the road when the first one was struck by a falling coconut. His friend, fearful that the turtle had lost his memory, rushed his companion to the hospital.

The next day, the friend came to consult the doctor. "How's his memory?" inquired the friend.

"He's cured," replied the doctor proudly. "In fact, I'm happy to report that he has turtle recall."

VINNY: My uncle's afraid his wife is going to be kidnapped.
MINNIE: What is he doing about it?
VINNY: He bought an Auntie-Theft (anti-theft) device.

Customer to hostess at a bed and breakfast lodging:

"Why does your dog growl at me while I'm eating? Does he want me to feed him?"

"No," said the hostess, "he's just angry because you're eating off his favorite plate."

Did you hear about the crook who hid out at a nudist camp? Nobody could pin a thing on him.

Did you hear about the fellow who was arrested for stealing street signs? He pulled out all the STOPS.

In a small town the chief of police, who was also the town veterinarian, was awakened from a sound sleep by a frantic caller.

"Please come quick!" said the woman.

"Do you need a cop or a vet?" he asked.

"Both," replied the woman. "We can't pry our dog's mouth open and there's a burglar's leg in it."

One day Mrs. Hennessey looked out at her driveway and saw her postman exchanging papers with a suspicious-looking man in dark glasses. When the man strode off, she confronted the postal worker with what she had seen. He then confessed that he was actually a spy for the CIA.

"You sure took a chance," said Mrs. Hennessey. "My dog is trained to attack strangers."

"There's no need to worry about that," the mailman reassured her. "He's one of us."

"I have such bad luck—when I put a seashell to my ear, I get a busy signal."

The absent-minded professor bought a new car and was worried he might forget what it looked like. His wife told him he could remember the license plate, 1492, just by thinking of Columbus.

Later that night, he stopped a stranger in the parking lot and said, "Excuse me, but can you tell me what year Columbus discovered America?"

THE CRIME IN OUR NEIGHBORHOOD IS SO BAD . . .

How bad is it?

The crime in our neighborhood is so bad that the local bank keeps its money in another bank.

The crime in our neighborhood is so bad that the candy store has a bouncer.

The crime in our neighborhood is so bad that the local gun shop had a back-to-school sale.

The crime in our neighborhood is so bad that the most popular form of transportation is the stretcher.

The crime in our neighborhood is so bad that the traffic lights say "Shoot" and "Don't Shoot."

The crime in our neighborhood is so bad that the doughnut shop closed down because the crooks kept stealing the dough.

The crime in our neighborhood is so bad that Boy Scouts help little old ladies across the street in armored tanks.

Mr. Bingsley went into a lumber supply yard and asked for some 2 × 4s.

"How long will you need them?" said the man in charge.

Thinking hard for a moment, Mr. Bingsley replied, "Well, I'm building a garage, so I'll need them for a long, long time."

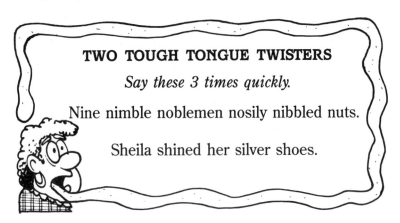

TWO TOUGH TONGUE TWISTERS

Say these 3 times quickly.

Nine nimble noblemen nosily nibbled nuts.

Sheila shined her silver shoes.

Disgusted with his life, an absent-minded professor decided to commit suicide. That night his wife returned home to find him hanging from the ceiling by his ankles.

"What are you doing up there?" she asked.

"I'm trying to kill myself," replied the professor.

"You're doing it all wrong," said his wife. "You're supposed to put the rope around your neck."

"I tried it that way," whined the professor, "but I couldn't breathe."

The absent-minded professor went fishing, but accidentally used aspirin instead of worms for bait. Not only did he catch a lot, but it was the first time a fish had been *hooked* on drugs.

A man who collected musical instruments went into an antique shop and spotted a large piano.

"This must be very old," said the man to the shopkeeper. "The keys are all yellow."

"Oh, no, sir," insisted the shopkeeper. "The piano isn't old, it's just that the elephant was a very heavy smoker."

A strange man walked into the post office with a lemon meringue pie stuck in one ear and cake in the other.

"Say, why do you have pie in one ear and cake in the other?"

"I'm sorry, you'll have to speak up," said the strange man. "I'm a little deaf."

MAY: How many terrorists does it take to replace a light bulb?

RAY: One hundred. One to screw it in and 99 to take the house hostage.

Did you hear about the farmer who bought some land 20 miles long and a foot wide? He wanted to grow spaghetti.

DOCTOR: Did you take my advice and sleep with the window open?
WOMAN: Yes, I did.
DOCTOR: Did you lose your cold?
WOMAN: No, but I lost my watch and handbag.

The police officer arrived at the scene of a grocery store holdup and said to the clerk who had been robbed, "You say the suspect helped himself to three bags of pretzels, the cash register and a pair of pants?"

"That's right, officer," said the clerk.

"I'm glad you didn't chase after him," said the cop.

"How could I?" replied the clerk. "They were my pants!"

A wife complained to her robber husband about their low income. "We're down to our last dollar," she said. "We need cash—and fast!"

"Okay, okay," grumbled her husband, "but you'll have to wait until the bank closes."

4. Furry Funny

Slim and Jim went duck hunting with their dogs for the first time. After a long day without much success, Slim remarked to Jim, "I think I figured out what we're doing wrong."

"What's that?" said Jim.

"We're not throwing the dogs high enough," said Slim.

NICKIE: What would you get if you crossed a golden retriever with a carrot?
DICKIE: A fetch-table.

DILL: How did your parakeet die?
WILL: Flu.
DILL: Don't be silly. Parakeets don't die from the flu.
WILL: Mine did. He flew under a bus.

Two hens were pecking around the yard when suddenly a softball came sailing over the fence, landing a few feet away from them.

Said the first hen to the second, "Gosh, will you just look at the ones they're turning out next door!"

A professor who collected birds went into an exotic pet shop and said, "I want a parrot that talks."

"I have just the parrot for you," said the owner, and he led the man to a cage where a very distinguished-looking parrot stood on a perch.

"Speak, Philmore!" said the pet shop owner.

Without missing a beat, Philmore spoke in a classically trained voice. "Where there's a will, there's a way. Crime doesn't pay. Money is the root of all evil."

"Pretty good, huh?" said the shopkeeper.

"How much?" said the professor.

"Three thousand dollars."

"Forget it," the professor said as he made his way to the door. "For that kind of money, I want a parrot that writes his own stuff."

A woman went to the pet shop to buy a parrot. When she picked out a rare breed, the owner congratulated her on her choice.

"If you'd like, I could send you the bill at the end of the month," said the pet shop owner.

"No, thanks," responded the woman, "I'll take the whole bird today."

A man bought a parrot, and for 20 years the bird kept silent, never uttering so much as a word. Every morning the parrot would wake up, stand patiently on its perch, and wait for its owner to come and feed it.

One morning, the man overslept. Using its beak, the parrot pried the cage door open, flew out, and perched on the man's head.

Pecking its owner's nose, the parrot squawked and said, "Excuse me, but it's nearly noon and I'm starved."

The man sat bolt upright. "Polly, you can talk!"

"Of course, I can talk," said the parrot.

"Then why haven't you said anything for 20 years?" asked the man excitedly.

"Because up till now," screeched the bird, "the service has been excellent!"

TERRY: You made a fool out of me!
JERRY: I can't take all the credit.

MEL: What do you give a seasick elephant?
NELL: Lots of space.

News Flash: "In a mysterious raid of a supermarket, thieves made off with 50 sacks of peanuts and 200 cartons of cigarettes. Police are on the lookout for an elephant with a persistent cough and yellow trunk."

HANK: Can you tell the difference between a miser and a sparrow?

FRANK: No, can you?

HANK: Of course. One's a little cheap, and the other's a little cheaper.

CAROL: Granddad finally got our puppy paper-trained.

DARRYL: Congratulations.

CAROL: Now if we could just get it to wait until Granddad finishes reading the paper.

FUZZY: My dog will only fly on the Concorde.

WUZZY: Why's that?"

FUZZY: He's a jet-setter.

Two hillbilly dogs went on vacation in the city. After finishing their business at a couple of fire hydrants, one of the animals spotted a row of parking meters and barked excitedly to his companion, "Look, Bob! Pay toilets!"

JUDY: I finally trained my dog not to beg at the table.
TRUDY: How did you do that?
JUDY: I let him taste my sister's cooking.

SIGN IN A VET'S OFFICE

**Be With You Shortly.
Sit. Stay. 'Atta Boy.**

When Oscar went away on vacation, his brother Harry promised to take care of his cat. The next day, Oscar called Harry to see how the animal was doing.

"Your cat is dead," said Harry, matter-of-factly.

"Dead?" said the shocked Oscar. "Why did you have to tell me like that?"

"How should I have told you?" asked Harry.

"Well," said Oscar, "the first time I called, you could have broken it to me gently. You could have said my cat was on the roof, but the fire department was getting her down. The second time I called, you could have told me the cat fell out of the fireman's arms and broke its neck. The third time I called, you could have said the vet did everything he could, but Fluffy passed away. That way it wouldn't have been so hard on me."

"I'm sorry," said Harry.

"That's all right. By the way, how's mother?"

"She's up on the roof," said Harry, "but the fire department is getting her down."

SYBIL: What's the difference between a powerful
jungle cat and a royal ruler who can't tell the truth?
BIBBLE: One is a king lion, the other is a lying king.

"Can you help me?" said the woman to the supervisor of the animal shelter. "I'm looking for a stray cat with one eye."

"Wouldn't you stand a better chance of finding him if you used both eyes?" suggested the supervisor.

THE WORLD'S SICKEST CAT JOKE

When the building caught fire, a woman appeared on the roof holding her pet cat in her arms.

"Throw the cat down!" yelled a man on the street.

"No, I can't," said the woman. "You might drop him."

"Trust me," the man reassured her. "I'm a goalkeeper for a professional soccer team."

Fearing for its life, the woman dropped the cat off the roof. The soccer player made a brilliant catch of the animal, then bounced it three times, and kicked it over the wall.

BORDEN: What's the difference between a person who dips baby sheep in paint and a dishonest beaver?
GORDON: One is a lamb dyer, the other a dam liar.

DAFFY: How can you tell when there is an elephant in your bed?
LAFFY: By the big E on his pajamas.

IGGY: What's big and grey with yellow feet?
ZIGGY: An elephant standing in a mustard jar.

SHAUNA: What is big and grey and goes in circles 50
  miles per hour?
WARNER: An elephant in a blender.

DING: What is big and grey and goes up and down, up
  and down?
DONG: An elephant on a bungee cord.

DINNY: What's big and grey and very dangerous?
GINNY: An elephant with an Uzi.

TEACHER: How can you tell the age of an elephant?
CLASS CLOWN: Count the candles on his birthday cake.

TEX: What has 12 tails, one horn and squeals?
LEX: A dozen pigs in a pickup truck.

A pig went to the bank for a loan to buy some trinkets for his new house.

"Hello, I'm Mr. Paddywhack," one of the bankers said. "How can I help you?"

When the pig explained, the banker frowned and said, "I'm sorry, but we never lend money to farm animals."

"Please," said the pig. "I promise I'll pay it back."

"Perhaps you'd better speak to the manager," insisted Mr. Paddywhack.

A few minutes later, the manager appeared and the pig again pleaded, "Please, all I need is a little money to buy some trinkets."

"I told him we don't lend money to livestock," the banker repeated.

"Oh, for goodness sake!" exclaimed the manager, throwing his hands up in the air. "It's a nick-nack, Paddywhack, give the hog a loan!"

DILLY: What has two horns and goes "Oom, oom"?
DALLY: A cow walking backwards.

NICK: Where do cows sleep?
SLICK: In cowabungalows.

LANCE: What's big, has a trunk and is blue all over?
VANCE: An elephant holding his breath.

SLIM: What's the difference between coffee and an
    elephant?
JIM: Elephants don't keep you up all night.

FRIP: When my father was in Africa, he chased
    elephants on horseback.
FRAP: Gee, I didn't know elephants could ride horses.

"Bet I can lift an elephant with six fingers."
    "Prove it."
    "Show me an elephant with six fingers and I'll be
glad to lift it."

A man went to the zoo for the first time and watched as the zookeeper fed a hungry four-legged animal.

"Gosh, I wonder what that wolf would say if he could talk," the man said to the zookeeper.

"He'd probably say, 'I'm a hyena, dummy,'" replied the zookeeper.

A woman went on a tour of the White House. As the guide led her down one of the historic halls, a door burst open and a large aquatic sea mammal, balancing a beach ball on its nose, scurried past.

"My, what was that?" exclaimed the woman.

"Oh, that's just the Presidential Seal," replied the guide.

TUTTI: What is grey, weighs three tons and soars through the air?
FRUTTI: A hippo on a hang glider.

A frog expert from the aquarium visited a third-grade class to give a talk on amphibians.

"It's easy to tell the male frogs from the female frogs," said the man, as he held up two cages. "When you feed them, the male frog will eat only female flies, and the female frogs will eat only male flies."

One boy in the back of the room raised his hand. "But how do you tell which flies are male and which are female?"

"How should I know?" replied the man. "I'm a frog expert."

Freddy went into a pet store and told the owner he wanted to raise goldfish. Picking out three fish from the tank, Freddy paid the man and took them home. A few days later he returned and said to the owner, "All my fish died."

The pet store owner gave Freddy three new fish and advised him to make sure the water was neither too cold nor too hot.

The next day Freddy was back with the news that the second batch of fish had died as well.

"I don't understand it," said the owner.

"I don't either," said Freddy. "I watered them with warm water, like you said. Maybe I'm just planting them too deep."

What am I?
I am not a plant, but I sometimes have leaves. What am I?
A table.

TODD: What animal can jump higher than the great pyramids?

ROD: Any animal—pyramids can't jump.

A woman walked into a pet shop and told the owner she needed two large rats and a dozen cockroaches.

"What do you need them for?"

"Because," said the woman, "I'm moving and my lease says that when I move I must leave the apartment in the same condition as I found it."

A father took his son to the zoo and showed him the tigers.

"Son," said the father, "if one of those tigers got out of its cage, it would tear me in two."

"If he does get out," replied the son, "what's the number of the bus I should take home?"

5. The Ghoul Next Door

WILLY: What would you get if you crossed a meat-eating dinosaur with a dictionary?

NILLY: A tyranno-thesaurus.

BERT: What would you get if you crossed a Tyrannosaurus Rex?

CURT: Eaten.

NIT: What do you call a masked man and his faithful dinosaur companion?

WIT: The Lone Ranger and Bronto.

WINNIE: What's Dracula's favorite sport?
VINNIE: Casketball.

Q. What would you get if you crossed a vampire with
an ancient Mexican civilization?
A. Bat Mayan.

CINDY: What do warlocks eat for breakfast?
MINDY: Deviled eggs.

"Hello, Operator, I'd like to speak to the Creature from
the Black Lagoon."
   "I'm sorry, but he's swamped right now."

FIRST MONSTER: How did Frankenstein's monster win
the election?
SECOND MONSTER: I guess he got all the volts.

GHASTLY GIFTS FOR HALLOWEEN

A new vampire doll. You wind it up and it starts coffin (coughin').

Build-It-Yourself King Tut Kit. Guaranteed or double your mummy back.

The Frankenstein Monster Assembly Kit. Head sold separately.

Ghostly Boomerang. It keeps coming back to haunt you.

FRANK: What did the monster say after the evil scientist cloned him.

HANK: Nothing, he was beside himself.

Starving for lunch, baby Godzilla wandered off and soon found himself at an army base watching a platoon of new soldiers line up for training. Scooping them up in his hand, he swallowed them all in a single gulp.

That night he complained to his mother of a belly ache.

"If I told you once, I told you a thousand times," she scolded, "stay away from raw recruits!"

Did you hear about the fortune-teller who did speed reading? She read instant tea.

While on a trip to a moon crater, the baby Martian's pet Zeebel ran away.

His parents searched the planetary terrain for hours, but they finally gave up.

"I want my Zeebel," cried the boy.

"I don't know where else it could be," said the father. "We already searched the dark side of the moon."

"Don't worry," the mother Martian reassured her son, "tomorrow we'll look on the bright side."

ZOEY: Why do zombies need to practice hard to make the soccer team?
JOEY: Because the competition is so stiff.

HY: Do you think it's possible to communicate with the dead?
CY: Well, you're certainly coming in loud and clear.

Little Jerome was on his way home from a friend's house one night when he realized that a werewolf was following him. He stopped to talk with the monster and it wasn't long before Jerome and the hairy beast were the best of friends.

When Jerome got home, he asked the werewolf to wait outside while he asked his mother if he could keep him as a pet.

"No, I won't allow that thing in the house!" said his mother. "It's full of fleas."

"I'm sorry," Jerome broke the news to the werewolf. "You'll have to stay out of the house—it's full of fleas."

Hotel clerk to witch: "Would you like a broom with a view?"

A man missed his bus and decided to walk home. He had journeyed several miles when night began to fall. Stumbling exhausted into a cemetery, the man laid down on the grass, rolled over, then slid into an open grave.

The next morning, an old woman arrived at the cemetery and, just as she approached the gravesite, she heard a voice murmur, "I'm so cold!"

Staring down into the grave, she replied, "Well, no wonder, you poor thing. You kicked all your dirt off."

KATE: Who entertains at ghost banquets?
NATE: An after-dinner spooker.

JEAN: What would you get if you crossed a vampire with a mummy?
DEAN: Either a flying bandage or a gift-wrapped bat.

Then there's the homeless mummy who was sent to jail. They say he got a bum wrap.

RANDY: When I was a boy, two huge purple monsters used to sleep one on top of the other in my room.
MANDY: Sounds like a lot of bunk to me.

Did you hear about the elevator operator who rode to the basement to pick up Dracula? He went down for the Count.

Benny had a curse put on him by an evil witch. The witch warned him that if he dared to use a razor on his face, his body would burn to a crisp. Benny, of course, didn't pay attention to the witch and one morning he got up and started to shave. No sooner had he touched the razor to his face when—POOF! His body went up in flames and he turned to ashes. *Moral:* A Benny shaved is a Benny burned.

6. Funny Frontiers

Have you heard the one about the cowboy who put super glue on his six-shooters? He always stuck to his guns.

A farmer who had never been on vacation decided to take a trip to the beach, but he accidentally ended up in the middle of the desert.

Stripping down to his bathing suit, he started to apply some sunblock, when a prospector drove up in a truck.

"I'm going swimming," said the farmer to the prospector.

"Swimming?" the prospector grunted. "But the ocean's 800 miles away from here!"

"Eight hundred miles!" exclaimed the farmer. "Wow, what a big beach!"

During a violent storm in the mountains, the prospector's cabin was completely covered by snow. The Red Cross Rescue Team launched a mission to save the poor man.

To reach the cabin, the rescue team flew by helicopter through a horrible blizzard. After landing, they trudged through dangerous snow drifts until they reached their destination. For several hours they worked to shovel away enough snow to clear the door.

When they finished, one of the rescue workers knocked on the door, announcing, "You can come out now. The Red Cross is here."

The door opened a crack and the grizzled prospector poked his head out. "Gee, I'm sorry," he said, "but I gave a pint last week."

RUNNING BEAR: My ancestors could dance and make it rain.
COWBOY: That's nothing. My folks can talk up a storm.

It was a peaceful day at the Black Horse Saloon when suddenly the doors swung open and in stormed Shaky Sam, the slowest gun in the West.

"All right," snarled Shaky, his face red with fury, "who done it? What nasty no-good varmint went and painted my horse purple?"

From the back of the saloon came the booming voice of Dangerous Dan, the fastest gunslinger in the West. "It was me, shrimpy," said Dangerous Dan, laying his fingers on his holster. "What are you going to do about it?"

"Oh, well, I was just wondering," stammered Shaky, "when—when are you going to give it a second coat?"

FIRST COWHAND: Why do you carry only one log for the campfire when the other hands carry two?

SECOND COWHAND: I guess because the others are too lazy to make two trips.

SASHA: What's the difference between a cowboy and a hangman?

NATASHA: One ropes a steer, the other steers a rope.

DIT: What would you get if you crossed a sheriff with a canary?

DOT: Wyatt Chirp.

CITY SLICKER: Well, I finally went for a ride this morning.

DUDE RANCH HAND: Horseback?

CITY SLICKER: Yep, he got back about an hour before I did.

MUTT: Did you hear about the cannibal horse?

JEFF: Don't be silly, horses don't eat other horses.

MUTT: This one ate his own fodder.

CLEM: Why do you suppose the sheriff fired the new hangman?

LEM: I reckon he was too slow learnin' the ropes.

"Wow!" said the city slicker as he watched a blacksmith put a horsehoe on the animal. "When you're through building that one, could you make me a horse, too?"

A group of city kids went on a field trip to a goat farm. As he watched them being herded, one of the boys noticed something strange about one of the goats.

"How come that goat doesn't have any horns?" said the boy to the goat herder.

"Well," said the herder, "some goats have their horns sawed off when they're young, others break them off while fighting. And sometimes horns fall off when they get old."

"What about that goat?"

"The reason that goat doesn't have any horns," replied the herder, "is because he's my dog."

Two buffaloes were grazing contentedly on the open prairie when a cowboy rode up. Looking the animals over, he shook his head and said, "You two are the ugliest buffaloes I ever saw. Look at you—your fur is tangled, you have humps on your backs and you slobber all over the place."

As the cowboy rode off, the first buffalo remarked to the second, "I think I just heard a discouraging word."

After seeing her first rodeo a little girl asked, "Daddy, what do cowboys get out of riding wild horses?" To which he replied, "Oh, I guess a couple extra bucks."

VANCE: What famous western sheriff started a chain of hotels?
LANCE: Hyatt Earp.

CHUCKIE: What's the difference between a physician who treats people on special occasions and Wyatt Earp's deputy?
DUCKIE: One's a holiday doc, the other's Doc Holliday.

The captain of a cavalry fort was eating dinner when his lieutenant burst through the door.

"Captain," he saluted, "I just received an urgent letter from our men in the desert outpost. They are greatly in need of water."

"Water supplies are due to arrive in a few days. Our men can wait," the captain assured him.

"I'm afraid they can't," said the lieutenant. "The stamp was attached to the envelope with a paper clip."

The dumbest cowboy in the West sauntered into a saloon and spotted a huge moose head on the wall. Impressed, he walked up to the saloon keeper and said, "Do you mind if I go into the next room and take a look at the rest of it?"

Two drivers of the midnight stage coach carried a sick passenger to the only doctor in the frontier town. They woke him up and said, "Doc, can you help this man?" "Sorry," said the sleepy doctor, "I only treat illnesses in the early stages."

7. Take My Parents, Please

Two sisters came home from school crying their hearts out.

"What's wrong with you both?" asked their mother.

The first sister started wailing, "All the kids at school ever do is make fun of my big feet."

"There, there," soothed the mother. "Your feet aren't that big." She turned her attention to the second sister. "Now why are you crying?"

"Because I've been invited to a ski party," weeped the second sister, "and I can't find my skis."

"That's okay," said her mother, "you can borrow your sister's shoes."

MOM: Why won't you take your sister to the zoo?
TOM: If they want her, they can come and get her!

Henry jumped for joy when his parents bought him two rabbits for his birthday. Although he played with them every day, the little bunnies soon proved a nuisance to Henry's parents. When not in their cage, they gnawed on the furniture and left rabbit droppings all over the house.

When one of the rabbits chewed up his slipper, Henry's father lost his temper.

"If that happens again," he shouted, "we're going to have one of those rabbits for dinner!"

"Gee, that's great," said Henry, his face lighting up. "Do you think I can teach him how to hold a spoon?"

DAUGHTER: Mom, where do eggs come from?
MOTHER: Hens.
DAUGHTER: Where does milk come from?
MOTHER: Cows.
DAUGHTER: Where do little celery plants come from?
MOTHER: The stalk brings them.

HE'S SO ABSENT-MINDED ...

How absent-minded is he?

He's so absent-minded he slammed his wife and kissed the door.

He's so absent-minded he poured maple syrup on his back and scratched his pancakes.

He's so absent-minded he reads the Monday morning paper to see if he was in an accident on Sunday.

He's so absent-minded he stood in front of the mirror for two hours trying to remember where he'd seen himself before.

He's so absent-minded he put tomato sauce on his shoe laces and tied knots in his spaghetti.

JASPER: My dad is so absent-minded instead of cornflakes he gave me soapflakes for breakfast.
CASPER: I bet that got you mad.
JASPER: Mad? I was foaming at the mouth.

"Mommy, Mommy, I swallowed a dictionary."
    "Don't breathe a word to your father."

IGGY: I have my mother's eyes, my mother's nose, and my mother's mouth.

ZIGGY: Gee, that doesn't leave much left of your mother.

"You can't have everything you want in life," the father explained to his son after learning the boy was in a fight at school. "Sometimes you must learn to give and take."

"The kid who beat me up must have gotten the same advice because he gave me a black eye and then took my lunch money."

DAD: There's something wrong with my shaving brush.

PAUL: That's strange. It worked fine yesterday when I painted my hot rod with it.

"Guess what we learned in school today, Mom," said Stanley as he burst through the front door. "We learned how to make babies."

"And how do you make babies?" said Stanley's mother.

"It's easy," replied Stanley. "First you change the *y* in baby to *i,* and then you add *es.*"

CHAD: Hey, Dad, look at this great watch I found in the street.

DAD: Are you sure it was lost?

CHAD: Of course it was lost. I saw the guy looking for it.

KARATE KID: Hey, Mom, I broke 600 boards today!

KARATE MOM: Son, must you always talk chop?

A mother scolded her son for not playing fair with his little brother.

"Why don't you let him play with your skateboard?"

"I have," said the boy. "I ride the skateboard down the hill, and he rides it up the hill."

A woman in a supermarket pushed a grocery cart with a screaming baby in it. As she moved up and down the aisles, she kept murmuring, "Stay calm, Rachel. Don't cry, Rachel. Don't scream, Rachel."

Another woman watched in admiration and then remarked, "You certainly have a lot of patience with little Rachel."

"What do you mean?" snapped the woman. "I'm Rachel!"

MOM: Quick, Hank, I've dropped my cake under the table. Don't let the dog get it!

HANK: Don't worry, Mom, I have my foot on it.

MOTHER: This morning there were two pieces of cake in this pantry and now there is only one. How do you explain that?

JUNIOR: I guess it was so dark that I didn't see the other piece.

"Daddy, daddy, there's a burglar in the kitchen, and he's eating mom's leftover stew."

"Go back to sleep. We'll bury him in the morning."

LYLE: My dad is so absent-minded.

KYLE: How absent-minded is he?

LYLE: He tried to teach me to swim by throwing me in the river.

KYLE: Did it work?

LYLE: It wouldn't have been so bad except for all the ice skaters.

SON: I have good news and bad news.

MOM: What's the good news?

SON: I captured a snake as long as the bathtub.

MOM: What's the bad news?

SON: It just escaped from the bathtub.

MOTHER: Remember—what do you do when you've had enough cake to eat at the birthday party?

JUNIOR: Come home?

SHE: Did I make the toast too dark, dear?

HE: I can't tell. The smoke is too thick.

DAD: Son, did I ever tell you the story about my forebears?

SON: No, but I heard the one about the three bears.

DAD: Why are you so late getting home?

VLAD: I stopped two kids from fighting.

DAD: How did you manage that?

VLAD: I beat them both up.

"Daddy, will you buy me a bass drum?"

"No way, it's noisy enough around this house."

"But I promise to play it only when you're asleep."

CHAD: My dad has an answering machine on his car phone.

BRAD: What does the message say?

CHAD: It says, "Hi, I'm at home right now, but if you'll leave your name and number, I'll call you when I'm out."

8. Homework Howlers

... YOU CAN TUNE A PIANO, BUT YOU CAN'T TUNA FISH!...

On the first day of class, Mrs. Spencer gave her lecture on bad behavior. "If there any troublemakers or loudmouths in this class, I want them to please stand up."

After a few moments of silence a shy little girl stood up.

"Do you consider yourself a troublemaker?" said Mrs. Spencer.

"No," replied the girl, "I just hate to see you standing there all by yourself."

TEACHER: Name the four food groups.
STANLEY: Fast, canned, junk and frozen.

THAT KID IN MY CLASS
IS SO DUMB...

How dumb is he?

That kid in my class is so dumb that mind readers only charge him half price.

That kid in my class is so dumb that he left his brain to science and science rejected it.

That kid in my class is so dumb that he once appeared on *Lifestyles of the Dull and Stupid.*

That kid in my class is so dumb that he once tried to pitch horseshoes but forgot to take them off the horse.

That kid in my class is so dumb that he paid $50 for a tattoo in the shape of a freckle.

HEALTH TEACHER: What's the best way to brush your teeth?

HEALTH CLOWN: With two hands.

HEALTH TEACHER: Why two hands?

HEALTH CLOWN: One hand to hold the toothbrush and the other hand to move your head from side to side.

TEACHER: If I had five potatoes, added three more potatoes, then divided by two potatoes, what would I have?

HENRY: Gosh, Teach, I was never too good at math (mashed) potatoes.

TEACHER: Do you think you can sleep in my class?

PUPIL: Well, I could if you didn't talk so loud.

JIM: What's the difference between a computer and a prison warden?

SLIM: One executes a program, the other programs an execution.

Woody got up in front of the class and read his book report aloud. When he finished, the teacher said, "That was very good, and I'm so glad you didn't tell us what happens at the end."

"Well," said Woody proudly, "I figured if they wanted to know the ending, they could do like I did and rent the video."

TEACHER: It took close to one hundred years to build one pyramid.

CLOWN: Must be the same contractor who's renovating our house.

TEACHER: Tony, please use the word "information" in a sentence.

TONY: Sometimes ducks fly information.

TEACHER: Stephanie, use the word "coincide" in a sentence.

STEPHANIE: Whenever it rains, I coincide to stay dry.

SUNDAY SCHOOL TEACHER: Why did Moses wander in the desert for forty years?

SUNDAY SCHOOL CLOWN: He was too stubborn to stop and ask for directions?

The meanest principal in the world was worried that his private school would close because of a lack of students. One day he called in his overworked assistant and demanded that he go out and recruit more students or be fired.

The next day five new students signed up. The day after that another ten signed up. Within a week the enrollment was sky high.

Pulling his assistant aside one day, the principal asked, "How did you get so many new students to sign up?"

"It was easy," replied the assistant. "I just started a rumor that you were quitting."

PRINCIPAL: Congratulations! Your son was finally promoted to third grade. How does he feel?

MOTHER: He was so excited he nicked himself shaving!

...NEXT YEAR I'LL BE ABLE TO CROSS THE STREET BY **MYSELF**!!

WOLVES

TEACHER: The law of gravitation explains why we stay on the ground.

LESTER: How did we stay on the ground before the law was passed?

TEACHER: Use the word "outwit" in a sentence.

HAROLD: My clothes get dirty every time I go outwit my friends.

SCHOOL NURSE: May I take your splinter out?

SCHOOL CLOWN: Yes, but be sure to have it back by midnight.

MATH TEACHER: If there are a dozen flies on the table and you swat one, how many are left?

MATH CLOWN: Uhhhh, just the dead one?

THE CRIME IN OUR SCHOOL IS SO BAD . . .

How bad is it?

The crime in our school is so bad that the class ring is a brass knuckle.

The crime in our school is so bad that if you're out sick, you have to bring a note from your parole officer.

The crime in our school is so bad that when the teacher says "Line up," she means a police lineup.

TEACHER: Timmy, give me a sentence using the word "diploma."

TIMMY: The bathtub was clogged, so I called diploma.

TEACHER: Joey, if you were facing east, what would be on your right hand?

JOEY: My fingers.

TEACHER: Sean, what is another name for a bunch of bees?

SEAN: A good report card.

TEACHER: Lenny, give me a sentence with the word "folder" in it.

LENNY: We should show respect folder people.

FOUR WAYS TO TELL WHEN SCHOOL CAFETERIA FOOD IS TERRIBLE

1) The mashed potatoes are so stale that you cut your finger on them.

2) They serve frogs for lunch and dissect hamburgers in science class.

3) You break a tooth eating a Jell-O cup.

4) Instead of knives and forks, you get hammers and crowbars.

A group of third-graders went on a field trip to visit some rock formations. After gazing at hundreds of stone walls, the teacher asked the class, "Where do you think all these rocks came from?"

"A great glacier brought them here," replied a small boy.

"Where is the glacier now?" said the teacher.

"It probably went back for more rocks," said the boy.

The principal called the mother of one of his students. He said, "I have good news and bad news. The bad news is your son thinks he's a frog."

"What's the good news?" asked the mother.

"The good news is I think we licked the fly problem in the cafeteria."

TEACHER: Horace, please use the word "tariff" in a sentence.

HORACE: My pants are so tight, they'll tariff I bend over.

MATT: Hey, Mother, guess what? Tomorrow there's a small PTA meeting.

MOTHER: What do you mean by small?

MATT: Just you, me and the principal.

TEACHER: Do you think Noah did a lot of fishing on the ark?

CLASS CLOWN: What, with only two worms?

NIBBLE NIBBLE

TEACHER: Luther, who was the first woman?

LUTHER: How should I know?

TEACHER: I'll give you a hint. It had something to do with an apple.

LUTHER: Oh, yeah, I know. Granny Smith!

TEACHER: Billy, please use the word "arrest" in a sentence.

BILLY: After pedaling up a steep hill on a bicycle, I sure needed arrest.

TEACHER: Hank, please use the word "column" in a sentence.

HANK: When I want to talk to a friend, I column up on the phone.

TEACHER: What did the colonists wear at the Boston Tea Party.

STUDENT: T-shirts?

SCIENCE TEACHER: What is the difference between electricity and lightning?

SCIENCE CLOWN: You don't have to pay for lightning.

TEACHER: Freddy, use the word "boycott" in a sentence.

FREDDY: Girls sleep in a girlcott while boys sleep in a boycott.

TEACHER: Dinah, use the word "decide" in a sentence.

DINAH: My dad got a flat tire so he pulled over to decide of the road.

TEACHER: Harvey, this is the third time this week you've been late.

HARVEY: I overslept.

TEACHER: Did you set the alarm?

HARVEY: That's the trouble. It goes off while I'm asleep.

SCIENCE TEACHER: Richard, what is HNO_3?

RICHARD: Uh, uh, let me see. It's on the tip of my tongue.

SCIENCE TEACHER: Well, in that case you better spit it out. It's nitric acid.

Suzie rushed into the school nurse's office, holding her hand and crying, "Ow! Ow!"

"What happened to you?" asked the nurse.

"I banged my fumb on the door," screamed Suzie.

"It's not 'fumb,' Suzie," the nurse corrected her. "It's pronounced *th*umb."

"Yes, miss," said Suzie. "And I hurt my thinger, too."

TEACHER: Why shouldn't you throw plastic bags into swamps in Louisiana?

CLASS CLOWN: Because the bags are not bayou degradable.

The art teacher instructed her students to draw a self-portrait. When Willy handed his in, the teacher took one look at it and said, "But, Willy, this isn't you."

"That's right," replied Willy. "It's a self-portrait of someone else."

MATH TEACHER: If I had 20 marbles in my right pocket, 20 marbles in my left pocket, 30 marbles in my right hip pocket, and 30 marbles in my left hip pocket, what would I have?
MATH CLOWN: Very heavy pants.

When the teacher gave the class a true-false test, Frank was ready for it. Reaching into his pocket, he dug out a coin and flipped it for each question. Heads for true and tails for false.

Later, when the rest of the class had gone off to lunch, Frank was still flipping the coins.

"What's taking you so long to finish?" asked his teacher.

"Oh, I finished a long time ago," said Frank. "Now I'm just checking my answers."

TEACHER: Alfred, please use the words "bitter end" in a sentence.
ALFRED: My mother bent over near my puppy and it bitter end.

9. You're Driving Me Crazy

Reassuring voice of airplane pilot:

"This is your captain speaking. I have good news and bad news. The bad news is we have just run out of fuel. However, the good news is I'm parachuting down to get help."

A hillbilly entered to race in the Indy 500, but came in dead last. The reason he was so slow was because he averaged five miles per hour and made 65 pit stops: three to get gas, two to change his tires, and 60 to ask directions.

Two guys named Bert were walking down the road when a big Mack truck hauling rocks came roaring past. As it drove over a bump, one of the bigger rocks slipped off the vehicle and squashed both men.

Rushing over to them, the truck driver pulled the rock away and then checked their wallets for identification.

A minute later a passerby pulled up and asked, "What happened here?"

"Woe is me" cried the truck driver. "I've killed two Berts with one stone!"

POLICE OFFICER: Can you explain why you were driving on the wrong side of the road?
OUT-OF-TOWNER: I certainly can. The other side was full.

TIP: I've started keeping my bicycle in my bedroom.
TOP: Why are you doing that?
TIP: I got tired of walking in my sleep.

Lem and Clem took a truck driving test. The first question they were asked by the examiner was, "What would you do if you were going down a hill and the brakes failed?"

Thinking long and hard, Lem finally blurted out, "Well, bein' as how Clem here would be takin' a nap, the first thing I'd do is wake him up."

"Why would you do that?" said the examiner.

"'Cause Clem ain't never seen a bad wreck before," Lem replied.

Two horse thieves were arrested by a posse of cowboys, who decided to hang them for their crimes. Unable to find any trees, the cowboys took the rustlers to a bridge and tied a rope around the first man's neck. Unfortunately, the rope broke and the thief fell into the river and swam off to safety.

As they tightened the noose around the second man's neck, he managed to stammer, "I sure hope this is a strong rope."

"Why's that?" asked one of the cowboys.

"Because," gulped the thief, "I can't swim."

Did you hear about the silly man who drove his truck off the cliff? He wanted to test his new air brakes.

A drag race driver spotted a puny boy on a bicycle and pulled up next to him.

"Hey, kid, wanna race?" said the driver, opening his door wide so he could check out the competition.

"Sure," said the boy.

The driver revved his engine and took off in a whirl of dust. Halfway down the block, out of the corner of his eye, he saw the cyclist rush past him. He stepped on the gas and took the lead, but a moment later the boy passed him again.

Finally pulling over, the driver rolled down his window and said, "Hey, how did you manage to keep up with me?"

"It was nothing," said the boy, exhausted and nearly out of breath. "My belt got caught in your door."

A woman got on a bus, but soon regretted it. The driver sped down the street, zig-zagging across the lanes, breaking nearly every speed limit in the country.

Unable to take it any longer, the woman stepped forward, her voice shaking as she spoke. "I'm so afraid of riding with you, I don't know what to do."

"Do what I do," said the bus driver. "Close your eyes."

A tourist driving down a deserted road came face to face with a sign that said: ROAD CLOSED. DO NOT ENTER. As the road ahead looked pretty good, he ignored the sign and drove on.

A few miles later he came to a bridge that was down. He promptly turned around and retraced his route. As he reached the point where the warning sign stood, he read the words on the other side: WELCOME BACK, STUPID!

A hillbilly and his mule were walking down the road when the hillbilly's friend drove up and said, "How about a lift to town?"

"Don't mind if'n I do," said the hillbilly. He hopped into his friend's truck while the mule ran behind. Soon they were going 55 miles an hour and the mule was right there, running alongside the truck. When the friend sped to 65, the mule still kept up with the truck.

At 80 miles per hour, the hillbilly's friend said, "I'm worried about your mule. His tongue is hangin' out."

"Which way is it hangin'?" asked the hillbilly.

"Right," replied the friend.

"Better stay in this lane, then," cautioned the hillbilly. " 'Cause he's about to pass."

JANIE: Daddy, if you don't buy me a fancy red sports car, I'll jump off a 300-foot cliff.

DADDY: Sounds like a big bluff to me.

Riding a bicycle built for two, a pair of sisters came upon a steep hill. Huffing and puffing, they finally reached the top, breathless.

"That," gasped the sister in front, "was a long climb."

"You're not kidding," sighed the other. "If I hadn't kept my hand on the brake, we would have rolled backwards!"

Seymour was riding his new bike down the street when he knocked over an old woman.

"You stupid, idiotic boy!" fumed the woman as she struggled to her feet. "Don't you know how to ride a bike?"

"Of course I do," replied Seymour. "I just don't know how to ring the bell."

EMMA: My teacher was in a car accident.
GEMMA: What happened?
EMMA: She was grading papers on a curve.

Three boys watched as a fire truck roared down the street. On top of the truck rode a beautiful Dalmatian, its nose pointing in the air.

Watching the majestic dog, the first boy observed, "They use him to pull the children to safety."

"That's not it," said the second boy. "Dalmatians are used to keep the people away from the fire."

"Both of you are wrong!" said the third boy.

"Oh, yeah?" snapped the other two. "Then what is he used for?"

"It's simple," replied the third boy. "They use him to find the fire hydrant."

A hillbilly hoisted his cow and his mule into the back of a trailer and hitched it to his pickup truck. A few miles down the road, the truck hit a bump, overturning the trailer and sending the hillbilly crashing through the windshield.

When a police officer arrived, he noticed the cow had broken both of its legs. Removing his gun from the holster, he put the poor thing out of its misery.

Next he noticed the mule's neck was broken and relieved the animal of its suffering as well.

Finally reaching the hillbilly lying on the side of the road, the officer waved his gun and said, "And how are you feelin'?"

Leaping to his feet, the hillbilly cried, "Nothing wrong with me, officer, I'm fine."

The absent-minded professor smashed his car into a parking garage and was thrown 30 feet. Dazed, but unhurt, he got up, straightened his tie and said to himself, "Now, I wonder where I parked the car."

MECHANICS INSTRUCTOR: What type of vehicle is useful for people with tired feet?
MECHANICS TRAINEE: A toe truck.

When their car broke down in the desert, Larry, Harry and Carey decided to go their separate ways for help.

Larry took the radiator out of the car so he could have water for his journey. Harry took the hubcaps off so he could use them to shield the sun from his face. Carey, however, removed the door from the car and started off down the road.

"Wait a minute," said Larry. "Why are you taking the door with you?"

"In case I need some air," replied Carey. "I can roll the window down."

The boy was excited the day he got his driver's license. No sooner had he sped off in his father's car when a police officer pulled him over for speeding.

"Can you identify yourself, young man?" said the police officer.

Nervously glancing at his reflection in the rear view mirror, he replied, "Yes, officer, that's me!"

Speeding down the highway at ninety miles an hour the man didn't realize he was caught in a radar trap. A secret camera recorded his vehicle and identified his car as exceeding the speed limit.

A few days later the man got a ticket in the mail along with a photograph of his car and the speed at which he was traveling.

So he mailed the ticket back with a picture of a $100 bill in it.

The hillbilly's wife had never driven a car in her life. One day her husband broke his leg and she was forced to drive him to the hospital in the city.

After traveling several bumpy miles, the hillbilly said to his wife from the back seat, "Are we gettin' closer to the city, Maddie?"

"We must be," replied Maddie. "I keep hitting more pedestrians."

The minister stopped in the middle of one of his powerful sermons to ask the question, "Who is God, anyway?"

At the back of the church, a little boy raised his hand. "God is a chauffeur," he said.

"Why do you say that?" asked the minister.

"Because," said the boy, "he drove Adam and Eve out of the Garden of Eden."

News Flash! A police van transporting prisoners collided with a cement truck. Officials are on the lookout for several hardened criminals.

A strange alien space ship landed at a gas station. The door opened and a three-eyed, tentacled thing got out and starting pumping gas into the ship.

The gas attendant noticed the letters "UFO" printed on the side of the spacecraft and curiosity got the best of him. "I'll bet that stands for "Unidentified Flying Object," he said to the attendant.

"No," replied the creature, "it stands for 'Unleaded Fuel Only.' "

10. Jock-Hilarity

Did you hear about the music lover who tried out for the Olympics? He's a compact disc thrower.

Did you hear about the goofy athlete who won a gold medal at the Olympics? He was so proud of it he had it bronzed.

A lawyer and his doctor friend were working out at a fitness center.

"I come here to exercise, but people always end up asking me for advice," complained the doctor to the lawyer. "What do you think I should do?"

"Simple," suggested the lawyer. "The next time you give them advice, send them a bill."

A few days later the doctor received a bill—from the lawyer!

A cricket walked into a London sporting goods store.

"Hey," said the clerk, surprised to see an insect with an interest in sports. "We have a game named after you."

"Really?" said the cricket modestly. "You have a game called Tyrone?"

HE'S PUT HONEY ON THE BAT!

THAT'S A STICKY WICKET!!

BASKETBALL PLAYER: Hey, coach, the doctor says I can't play basketball.
BASKETBALL COACH: I could have told you that.

TEACHER: Name the four seasons.
CLASS CLOWN: Baseball, basketball, football and hockey.

TRACK STAR (*to mother*): "Hey, Mom, how about a sandwich before the race?"
MOTHER: "Absolutely not. It isn't polite to eat and run."

Ed, Ned and Fred went to the Summer Olympics, but soon discovered that all the events were sold out. "I have an idea," said Ed. "Let's pose as athletes and they'll have to let us in."

The three agreed it was a good idea and Ed decided to go first. Running across the street to an old junk site he found a cast-iron roller. Lugging it in his hands he grunted and went past the security guard saying, "Williams, shotput," and was admitted.

Next, Ned ran to the same site and picked up a length of metal tubing. "Harris, pole vault," he announced, and the guard waved him on.

Determined to follow his friends, Fred searched and searched the area until he discovered a roll of barbed wire. Striding up to the guard, he announced in a confident voice, "Johnson, fencing."

JAKE: Our town's baseball league is the worst.
JOCK: How bad is it?
JAKE: It's so bad the kids throw away the baseball cards and collect the gum.

CHUCKIE: Did you hear about the trapeze artist who fell to the ground?
DUCKIE: Did he hit a net first?
CHUCKIE: Yes, and Annette wasn't too happy about it.

Then there was the baseball player who went to church twice a day because he kept hoping for a double pray.

ZIP: I saw someone hit a grand-slam home run with no men on base.
ZAP: That's impossible!
ZIP: Not when your watching a girls' softball game it isn't.

"I bet I can run faster than you can," bragged Hank to his friend Bill one day.

"I bet you can't," replied Bill.

To prove his point Hank took Bill to the roof of the biggest building in town, nearly 30 stories high. Hank removed his watch and, holding it over the edge of the building, let it drop. Quickly, in a whirl of dust, Hank dashed down the steps and moments later, reaching ground level, held out his hand and caught the watch in it.

Signaling that it was his turn, Bill removed his watch and let it fall. Taking his time, he strolled to the elevator and pushed the button. A few minutes later the elevator appeared and, after stopping at several floors, finally arrived on the first floor. Stepping into the lobby, Bill stopped to get a soda from the vending machine, then calmly walked outside just in time for the watch to drop neatly into his hands.

"Hey, that was amazing!" remarked Hank. "How did you do it?"

"Simple," said Bill. "My watch is five minutes slow."

There's so much traffic in our gym
the stationary bicycles
have rear view mirrors.

NIT: What's the difference between a baseball announcer and an abusive dog owner?

WIT: One spots the hit, the other hits the Spot.

The rookie parachute jumper took a deep breath and prepared to jump from the plane.

"Don't forget—if the first cord fails to operate, pull the backup cord," the instructor reminded him. "Ready?"

"Ready!" said the jumper. He leaped from the plane, counted to ten, then pulled the cord. When nothing happened he pulled the backup cord. Still nothing.

As he plummeted helplessly to earth, a woman suddenly flew past him towards the sky.

"Hey!" he shouted. "Do you know anything about parachutes?"

"No," replied the woman, "do you know anything about gas stoves?"

LENNY: What would you get if you crossed a computer, a slob and an Olympic athlete?
BENNY: A sloppy (floppy) discus thrower.

A horse walked up to the racetrack betting window and plopped his money down.

"I want to bet fifty dollars on myself to win the fifth race," said the horse.

"I can't believe this!" said the astonished clerk.

"You can't believe what?" said the horse. "That I can actually talk?"

"No," replied the clerk. "I just don't think you have a snowball's chance in July of winning the fifth race."

EDDIE: Coach, where am I on the tug-of-war team?
COACH: You're the third jerk from the left!

A boy's father scolded him for breaking a neighbor's window with a baseball. "What did he say to you when you broke it?" asked the father.

"Do you want to hear what he said with or without the bad words?"

"Without, of course!"

"Well, then he said nothing."

A man left with his friends for the golf course early in the afternoon, promising his wife he would be back in time for dinner.

Nine o'clock that night the husband returned from the golf course, exhausted and shaken.

"Why were you so late?" asked the wife.

"It was awful," replied the husband. "Harry died on the fifth hole."

"How terrible!" exclaimed his wife.

"It was," said the husband. "For the rest of the game it was hit the ball, drag Harry, hit the ball, drag Harry . . ."

Two aliens from outer space landed on a golf course and watched with great curiosity as a golfer hit a ball into the high grass. Frustrated and mumbling loudly to himself, the golfer stumbled into the grass and retrieved the ball.

Next he hit the ball into a big sand pit, cursing and shouting furiously.

Finally, he hit a perfect hole in one. The first alien groaned and said to the second, "Uh-oh, cover your ears; he's in real trouble now."

Ernie and Bernie put on their ice skates and ventured out onto a frozen lake.

After skating in circles for a while, Ernie stopped and said to Bernie, "Say, do you think there are ducks out here?"

"Of course not," said Bernie. "They all flew south for the winter."

"Well, in that case," replied Ernie in a panic-stricken voice, "I think the ice is quacking."

CINDY: I can't believe you took your blind grandfather sky diving.
MINDY: He really enjoyed it.
CINDY: Do you plan to take him again?
MINDY: No way!
CINDY: But if he liked it, why not?
MINDY: Well, he enjoyed it, but his seeing-eye dog wasn't too crazy about it.

Did you hear about the second-string football player who flooded the stadium with water? He was hoping the coach would send him in as a sub.

Did you hear about the athlete who was so stupid that when he earned his varsity letter somebody had to read it to him?

TEACHER: What is the meaning of "behold."
JOKER: It's what one bee wrestler uses to pin another bee wrestler.

After driving all night a man pulled over to the side of the road to get some rest. Before long there was a rap on the window and a jogger standing there.

"Pardon me," said the jogger, "but do you have the correct time?"

"Six A.M." the man replied groggily, and then went back to sleep.

A few minutes later another jogger tapped on the window.

"Hate to bother you, but do you have the time?"

"Five after six," the man growled angrily, scaring the second jogger off.

Deciding to put a end to the disturbances, the man made a sign saying, "I DO NOT HAVE THE TIME" and hung it on the window.

Soon, awakened by yet another tapping on the window, the man rolled down the window and saw a third jogger.

"I saw your sign," said the jogger, cheerfully pointing to his watch. "It's half past six!"

"I don't understand you, Skeets," said the Little League coach to one of his slower players. "The distance between first and second base is exactly the same as the distance between second and third base. Yet it took you longer to get from second to third. What's your excuse?"

"Gee, coach," replied Skeets, "everyone knows there's a shortstop between second and third."

RON: What would you get if you crossed a karate
     instructor with a wheelbarrow?
LON: A chopping cart!

ABE: What would you get if you crossed a baseball player with a Boy Scout?

GABE: I don't know, but I bet he sure could pitch a tent.

FLIP: My sister is so dumb she thinks a football coach has four wheels.

FLOP: That is pretty dumb. How many wheels does it have?

A hunter got lost in the woods. After wandering in the forest for three days, exhausted and starving, he spotted a forest ranger coming towards him.

"Thank goodness you found me!" said the relieved hunter. "I've been lost for three days!"

"You think that's bad?" replied the ranger. "I've been lost for two weeks."

11. No Biz Like Show Biz!

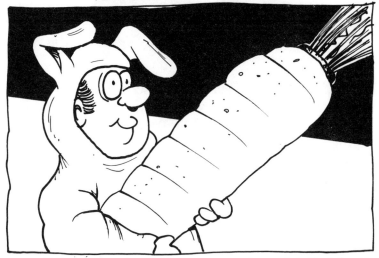

NED: What comedy team eats carrots and tells jokes?
TED: Rabbit and Costello.

LOONY: What would you get if you crossed a famous cartoon team with a star?
TOONY: Rocky and Bulltwinkle.

Did you hear about the new TV series called *Flashback*? It's a half hour show and goes from 9:00 to 8:30.

The son of a famous TV star showed his mother his report card.

"I hope you did well," his mother said hopefully, opening the envelope.

"You bet I did," replied the son. "In fact, my teacher has signed me to do another 13 weeks this summer."

For several years the man trained his dog to tell jokes and sing songs. One day he got the dog his first break, a spot on the *Tonight Show.* When the dog came on stage, however, he froze and didn't say a word.

On the way home, the man scolded the dog. "We had a shot at stardom and you blew it. What happened?"

"I couldn't see the darn cue cards," growled the dog.

Two ants wandered inside a large-screen television set. After crawling around for hours the first ant started crying, "I think we're lost, I think we're lost!"

"Don't worry, we'll get out," said the second ant confidently. "I brought along a TV Guide."

IKKY: What has four heads, runs forward and
    backwards very fast and loves to play?
CHICKIE: A VCR.

DAD: How's that video correspondence course going?
CHAD: I'm learning the three R's.
DAD: What are they?
CHAD: Reviewing, Rewinding, and Recording.

A woman in a movie theater approached a man sitting in one of the front rows. "Excuse me," said the woman, "but did a dumb blonde just spill soda all over your shirt?"

"Why, yes, she did," replied the man.

The woman turned and shouted up the aisle, "Hey, Shirley, I found our seats!"

Did you hear about the trombone player who got kicked out of the school band? He kept letting things slide.

JUDGE: You are accused of hitting a comic with your car and dragging him seven blocks.
DRIVER: It was eight blocks, Your Honor.
JUDGE: Don't you think that's carrying a joke too far?

NIT: I got a bad case of frostbite at the drive-in movie.
WIT: What did you go to see?
NIT: "Closed for the Winter."

MASON: What invincible warrior has a dome-shaped head?
JASON: Conehead the Barbarian.

A boy was taken to the ballet by his mother. As the program began, the boy leaned over his seat and whispered, "Mom, they're all dancing on their toes."

"Yes, I know," shushed his mother. "That's the way they do it."

The boy watched for a moment longer and then said, "Well, why don't they just get taller dancers?"

SCIENCE TEACHER: Today, class, we're going to see a film about waterfowl.

SCIENCE CLOWN: Oh, no, not another duckumentary!

Did you hear about the goose that watched a horror movie and got people-bumps?

Did you hear there's a new movie about a dentist who goes back and forth in time? It's called *Plaque to the Future.*

A hillbilly moved to the city and went to his first movie.

"I'll have one ticket, please," he said to the girl in the glass booth.

"But that's the third ticket you've bought in five minutes," said the girl.

"I know," replied the hillbilly, "but before I get in the door some jerk keeps tearing them in half!"

KURT: What would you get if you crossed a swimming pool with a movie house?

BERT: A dive-in theatre.

BEST SELLERS FROM
THE VIDEO SHELF

Attack of the Flying Blood Suckers
Starring Amos Quitoe

The Last Woman on Earth
Starring Emma Lone

Revenge of the Tiger
Starring Claude Body

Prison Break
Starring Freda Convict

It's Coming to Get You!
Starring Sue Nora Later

Police Beat
Starring Laura Norder

Diary of a Mad Kidnapper
Starring Caesar Quick

Trapped in the Arctic
Starring I.C. Waters

My Three Years in Second Grade
Starring Dee Moted

Something Fishy
Starring Ann Chovie

Samson Brings Down the House
Starring Rufus Falling

What would you get if you crossed the Greatest Show on Earth with the Ice Capades?

A three-rink circus.

A man brought a rabbit, a frog and a chicken to a talent agent's office. As the agent watched with disinterest, the frog drank from a glass of water while the rabbit danced around the chicken and performed somersaults.

Just as the agent was about to toss the man and his animals out the door, the rabbit took a bow and said, "Thank you and goodnight!"

"That's incredible!" said the agent. "The hare is hired."

"But what about the frog?" said the man.

"The frog has no talent, I want the rabbit," replied the agent.

"But the chicken—" said the man.

"No chicken, I want the rabbit!" the agent insisted.

The next week the agent got the rabbit a spot on a TV variety show. When it was introduced, the rabbit hopped on stage, cleared its throat, and then quietly walked off.

"What happened?" said the agent to the owner. "The rabbit didn't talk!"

"Talk?" said the owner. "The rabbit doesn't talk."

"But last week in my office I heard it—"

"I tried to tell you."

"Tell me what?"

"About the chicken. He's a ventriloquist."

12. Open Wide and Say Ha!

When it was time for his wife to have their child, the husband quickly called the hospital.

"My wife's in labor," said the man, unable to contain his excitement.

"Calm down," said the dispatcher. "Is this her first baby?"

"No," he replied. "This is her husband."

A man who had lived a long and happy life was lying on his deathbed when the aroma of his wife's chocolate chip cookies filled the air.

"My time has come," said the old man when his wife stepped into the room. "But before I die, I would like to have one last nibble of your delicious chocolate chip cookies."

"I'm afraid that's out of the question," answered his wife. "Those are for the family after the funeral."

A man stubbed his toe so badly he decided to go to the doctor. When he arrived at the office, the nurse directed him to remove his clothes and wait in the next room.

"I just hurt my toe," complained the man. "Why do I need to take off my clothes?"

"Everyone who sees the doctor has to undress," explained the nurse. "It's our policy."

"Well, I think it's a stupid policy! Making me undress just to look at my toe!"

From the next room, another man's voice piped in, "That's nothing! I just came to fix the telephone."

WILL: Why did the rubber woman from the circus enter therapy?

DILL: She was all bent out of shape.

PATIENT: It's been one month since my last visit and I still feel miserable.

DOCTOR: Did you follow the instructions on the medicine I gave you?

PATIENT: I sure did. The bottle said "Keep tightly closed."

FIRST PATIENT: My doctor is really nice to me.

SECOND PATIENT: How nice is he?

FIRST PATIENT: When he treated me for double pneumonia, he only billed me for one pneumonia.

DIT: My doctor told me to take something good for my cold.

DOT: What did you take?

DIT: I took his coat.

A man went to a psychiatrist and brought his entire family with him.

"Help us, doc," said the man. "We all think we're elephants. What should we do?"

"For starters," replied the doctor. "You can stop holding each other's tails."

My doctor is so slow his waiting room couch opens up into a sleeper.

WIFE: Doctor, my husband was run over by a steamroller. What should I do?

DOCTOR: Tell him to stay flat on his back.

HUSBAND: Doctor, my wife thinks she's a pretzel. What should I do?

DOCTOR: Tell her to cut down on her salt.

STRESSED WIFE: Doctor, my husband thinks he's a satellite dish.

DOCTOR: Don't worry, I can cure him.

STRESSED WIFE: I don't want him cured, I want him adjusted. I can't get the movie channel.

When he read the Surgeon General's report that smoking caused cancer in rats, Harvey gathered up all the cigarettes in the house and put them on a high shelf so his rats couldn't reach them.

Orville went to his doctor for a checkup. When the doctor asked him to describe his eating habits, Orville replied, "For breakfast, I have a gallon of grape juice, a liter of prune juice and six bowls of oatmeal. Then I finish up with eight croissants, half a dozen eggs and a cup of coffee. For lunch I have a can of Spam, a pot of soup, a pound of cole slaw, a dozen doughnuts and a cup of coffee. For supper I start with a ten-pound lobster, a meatloaf, some stew, a turkey, a loaf of bread and finish up with apple pie à la mode and a cup of coffee."

"Good heavens!" exclaimed the doctor.

"I know what you're going to say, doc," said Orville. "You think I'm drinking too much coffee."

DOCTOR: I've got good news and bad news. Which would you like to hear first?

PATIENT: The bad news.

DOCTOR: The bad news is we have to remove both your legs.

PATIENT: What's the good news?

DOCTOR: The good news is the man in the next bed wants to buy your shoes.

PATIENT: Can you tell me how to live in the present?
DOCTOR: Yes, but not right now.

WIFE: Doctor, doctor, my husband thinks he's a
    shepherd!
DOC: Don't lose any sheep over it.

MOTHER: Doctor, doctor, my son thinks he's a parking
    meter.
THERAPIST:Will he see me?
MOTHER: If you put a quarter behind his ear, he will.

Boy to X-ray technician after swallowing a quarter:
"Do you see any change in me?"

NIT: This ointment is making my legs smart.
WIT: Quick, rub some on your head!

PATIENT: Thanks to your help, doctor, I no longer
    think I'm a Labrador retriever. How can I ever
    repay you?
DOCTOR: For starters, you can fetch me some lunch.

SIGN IN A VISION CENTER WINDOW

> **If you don't see exactly what you want, you've come to the right place.**

HUSBAND: My wife talks to her plants.
DOCTOR: What's wrong with that?
HUSBAND: On the telephone?

PATIENT: I'm cured, I'm cured! I no longer think I'm a dog.
DOCTOR: Are you sure?
PATIENT: If you don't believe it, feel my nose.

The absent-minded professor arrived at the emergency ward with both of his ears badly burnt.

"How did this happen?" asked the doctor.

"I was ironing my shirt," explained the professor, "when the phone rang and I answered the iron by mistake."

"What about the other ear?"

"That happened when I called for an ambulance."

GEORGE: What are the side effects of this drug?
DOCTOR: You'll sprout whiskers and lose your appetite.
GEORGE: Oh, well, hair today, gaunt tomorrow.

NURSE: Doctor, doctor, the man you just treated collapsed on the front step. What should I do?
DOCTOR: Turn him around so it looks like he was just arriving.

Patient to Hospital Administrator:
  "I'm here to file a complaint."
  "What's the complaint?"
  "The doctor used a four-letter word during surgery."
  "What word was that?"
  "Oops!"

Did you hear about the duck who's a plastic surgeon? His motto is "Pay now, bill later."

Did you hear about the absent-minded Siamese twins? Everything goes in one ear and out the brother.

Did you hear about the guy who's so lazy, he hires other people to walk in his sleep?

NIT: I just had ten cavities taken care of.
WIT: I guess you had your fill.

NORA: What's the difference between a sewage plant and a sit-up?

DORA: One is good for waste treatment, the other's good for treating your waist.

A man rushed into an emergency room of a hospital and asked an intern for a cure for hiccups. Grabbing a glass of water, the intern quickly splashed it into the man's face.

"What did you do that for?" exclaimed the man.

"You don't have the hiccups any more, do you?" said the intern.

"No," replied the man. "My wife out in the car has them."

STUFFY: Doctor, how can I keep my chest cold from going to my head?

DOCTOR: Try tying a knot in your neck.

WILLY: Doctor, everyone tries to take advantage of me. What should I do?

DOCTOR: Give me two hundred dollars and let me borrow your car.

When Jimmy came home from the dentist his mother was shocked at how much the bill was.

"You said it would only cost 60 dollars," she said to the dentist on the phone. "Why is the bill for 240 dollars?"

"It is usually 60," explained the dentist. "But Jimmy screamed so loud he scared off three of my other patients."

PATIENT: I feel nauseated, doctor. Can you help me out?

DOCTOR: Certainly, use the door right behind you.

DOCTOR: How are those strength pills I gave you last week working?

CLEM: I don't know. I'm not strong enough to get the cap off the bottle yet.

Did you hear about the man who fell into an upholstery machine? He's fully recovered.

CHLOE: Last night my computer died.

ZOEY: What did it die of?

CHLOE: A terminal illness.

PATIENT: Doctor, doctor, I keep thinking I'm the Abominable Snowman.
DOCTOR: Sorry, I don't get your drift.

ZIGGY: My sister thinks she's a cigarette.
DOCTOR: Well, bring her in.
ZIGGY: I can't, this is a no-smoking building.
DOCTOR: In that case, put her out.

PSYCHIATRIST: What do you dream about?
STANLEY: Playing major league baseball.
PSYCHIATRIST: That's it? No dreams about girls, cars or food?
STANLEY: What, and miss my turn at bat?

DEXTER: Tell me, Doc, how serious is it?
DOC: Well, if I were you, I wouldn't get into a long chess match.

Wise Man Says

You can't have everything. Where would you put it?

Carry a rabbit in a storm and the wind'll blow the hare in your face.

PATIENT: Doctor, I feel like a butterfly!
DOCTOR: Have you always felt this way?
PATIENT: No, a few years ago I felt like a caterpillar.

Since old Mr. Willoughby was allergic to cold medicines, his doctor advised him to drink a large glass of carrot juice after a long bath.

A week later when Mr. Willoughby returned, his doctor asked him how he had done. "Not too good," the old man replied. "After I drank the hot bath, I didn't have room for the carrot juice."

LOU: How is a hobo different from a non-smoking goat?
STU: One smokes butts, the other butts smokers.

"My sister ate some bad chicken at the mall yesterday."

"Croquette?"

"Not yet, but the doctors are keeping an eye on her."

SANDY: I bet I can tell you what everyone in the world is doing at this very moment.

ANDY: Oh, yeah, what?

SANDY: Growing older.

A man rushed into his doctor's office and cried, "My hair is falling out! Can you give me something to keep it in?"

"Certainly," said the doctor reassuringly, handing the man a small box. "Is this big enough?"

The man arrived at his doctor's office anxious to hear the results of his hospital tests. "I have bad news and terrible news," said the doctor.

"What's the bad news?" said the man.

"The bad news is you have only 48 hours to live."

"What's the terrible news?"

"I left a message on your answering machine two days ago."

A mother complained to her doctor about her daughter's strange eating habits. "All day long she lies in bed and eats yeast and car wax. What will happen to her?"

"Eventually," said the doctor, "she will rise and shine."

13. Court Shorts

A woman frantically dialed 911. "You've got to help me," she said. "I've lost my dog!"

"Sorry, miss," said the dispatcher, "but we don't handle missing animals."

"But you don't understand. This is no ordinary dog. He can talk."

"Well, you better hang up, he might be trying to call in."

HARRY: My uncle's with the FBI.

LARRY: Is that so?

HARRY: Yes, they picked him up trying to leave the country.

Knock-knock!
  Who's there?
CIA.
  CIA who?
C, I Ate the whole cake!

VERN: Did you hear about the depressed prisoner?
FERN: What was his problem?
VERN: He was down, but not out.

A poor peasant was wandering through Sherwood Forest when suddenly a man rode up and dropped a bag of gold coins into the peasant's hands.

"Who are you?" asked the astonished peasant.

"I'm Robin Hood," replied the rider. "I steal from the rich and give to the poor."

"Yippee!" cried the peasant. "I'm rich! I'm rich!"

Taking out his sword, Robin Hood pointed it at the man and said, "Rich, huh? In that case, hand over the money!"

JUDGE: Weren't you once up before me?
CROOK: Couldn't have been me, I'm a late riser.

Two crooks arrived in a prison cell at the same time.
"Hey, how long you in for?" asked the first man.
"Thirty years," replied the second man. "How about you?"
"Thirty years and a day," said the first. "So since you're leaving first, why don't you take the bed closest to the door?"

NILLY: What do gangsters put on the front of the car?
WILLY: A hood ornament.

JUDGE: You are accused of stealing garments from the clothesline of a convent. What do you have to say for yourself?
CROOK: I promise I won't make a habit of it.

LENNY: According to motor vehicle statistics, a man gets hit with a car every 38 minutes.

BENNY: If I were him, I'd stay off the street!

Lawyer to Defendant:

"Do you wish to challenge any of the jury members?"

"Well, I think I could lick that little guy on the end."

BRENDA: What's the difference between a counterfeit bill and a rabbit with mental problems?

GLENDA: One is bad money, the other is a mad bunny.

Stanley borrowed ten dollars from his friend Ziggy, and promised to pay it back. A few days later Stanley and Ziggy were walking down the street when a mugger leaped in front of them shouting, "Give me all your money or I'll shoot!"

Digging into his pocket, Stanley pulled out a ten and handed it to Ziggy. "Here's the ten dollars I owe you," he said.

A cop pulled a man over for speeding. Thinking quickly, the man said to the officer, "It's an emergency. My mother's in the back seat. She took an overdose of reducing pills."

Checking the back seat, the officer shook his head. "I don't see anyone back there."

"Oh, no!" cried the man. "I'm too late!"

JUDGE: I hereby sentence you to prison for the rest of your life.

CROOK: Rest? Thanks, Your Honor, I could use a rest.

A frightened man dialed 911 to report an assault.

"I was coming in the back door," said the man to the dispatcher, "when I was struck on the head. Luckily, I got into the house and locked the door. Please send help."

After advising him to stay calm, the dispatcher sent a rookie cop to investigate. A half hour later the rookie returned to the station with a large bump on his head.

"That was fast work," remarked the police chief. "How did you do it?"

"It was easy," replied the rookie, rubbing his sore head, "I stepped on the rake, too."

FIRST CROOK: Would you like to share a taxi with me?

SECOND CROOK: Sure.

FIRST CROOK: Okay, you get the tires, I'll get the hubcaps, you get the radio, I'll get the battery . . .

SHERLOCK HOLMES: Why are you taking art classes, Watson?

DR. WATSON: So I can draw my own conclusions, Holmes.

The warden of the prison felt sorry for one of his inmates. Every weekend on visitor's day while most of the prisoners were visited by family and friends, poor George sat alone in his cell.

One visiting day the warden called George into his office. "I notice you never have any visitors, George," said the warden, putting a comforting hand on George's shoulder. "Tell me, don't you have any friends or family?"

"Oh, sure I do, warden," replied George cheerfully. "But they're all in here."

The absent-minded professor stood in the middle of a busy intersection while the policeman directed traffic.

"Excuse me, officer," said the confused man, "but can you tell me how to get to the hospital?"

"Certainly," said the officer. "Just keep standing there."

FLO: Hey, did you hear the cops are looking for a man with a hearing aid?

JOE: Why don't they use police dogs?

A cop gave a woman a speeding ticket.

"And what am I supposed to do with this?" said the woman in a huff.

"Save it," said the cop. "When you collect four of them, you get to ride a bicycle."

The private detective had just moved into his new office when he heard a knock at the door. Hoping to make a good impression on his first customer, he yelled, "Come in!" and then picked up the telephone and pretended he was talking to someone important.

The visitor waited patiently. Finally, the detective hung up the phone and said, "As you can see, I'm very busy. What can I do for you?"

"Not much," said the man. "I'm here to hook up your phone."

ROBY: Knock-knock!
TOBY: Who's there?
ROBY: Amen.
TOBY: Amen who?
ROBY: Amen trouble with the law.

A police officer was escorting a prisoner to jail when his hat blew off down the sidewalk.

"Shall I run and get it for you?" said the prisoner.

"You must think I'm really stupid!" said the officer. "You wait here and I'll get it."

A crook pleaded to the judge:

"Your Honor, I'm not guilty. I can prove it if you just give me some time."

"My pleasure," replied the judge. "Twenty years. Next!"

TED: How many judges does it take to change a light bulb?
NED: Beats me.
TED: Two. One to turn it and one to overturn it.

Rotten Ralph was always getting into trouble for stealing candy. One day he was caught red-handed and the police officer decided to teach him a lesson. He put Rotten Ralph in a jail cell for a few hours with a notorious criminal.

"What are you in for, kid?" asked the hood.

"I stole some candy," replied Rotten Ralph.

"Why didn't you rob a bank like me?" said the crook.

"Because I don't get out of school until three o'clock," explained Rotten Ralph.

14. All Worked Up!

MOE: What do an army private and a waitress have in common?

JOE: They both take orders all day long.

Daffy Dan was out of work and needed money. He asked his best friend, Dudley, if there were any odd jobs he could do.

"As a matter of fact there are," said Dudley. "Go into the garage, get a can of green paint and paint my porch."

A few hours later Dan knocked on Dudley's door.

"Well, it's done," beamed Dan proudly. "Except you were wrong about one thing. It's not a Porsche, it's a Ferrari."

MATILDA: Mommy, tell me the story about the castle
    ditch digger who fell asleep on the job.
MOTHER: He was de-moated.

News Flash: A midget psychic robbed the First National
Bank and made off with all the cash. The police say the
small medium is still at large.

Then there was the dumbest bank robber in the
world. He put a paper bag on his head and told the
teller to put all the money in the stocking.

But he may not have been as dumb as the robber who
stole a thousand dollars from a bank and then went
to the next window and said, "I'd like to open an
account."

Did you hear about the nose-drop salesman who kept insisting people try his product? He was fired for sticking his business into other people's noses.

Goofy George saw an advertisement for a handyman for an apartment complex and decided to apply for the job.

"What do you know about plumbing?" was the interviewer's first question.

"Nothing," said George.

"What about electricity?"

"Not a thing."

"How about landscaping?"

"Never cut a lawn in my life."

"Then tell me," said the baffled interviewer, "just what makes you so handy?"

"I live right around the corner," said George.

Stanley got a job painting the yellow stripes on the highway. His first day he dipped his brush into the bucket and managed to paint an entire mile of yellow lines. The second day he painted half a mile. The third day a quarter of a mile.

On the fourth day Stanley's boss showed up and asked, "How come each day you seem to paint less and less?"

"Well, sir," explained Stanley, "that's because each day I get farther and farther away from the bucket."

Two stooges named Benny and Lenny got a job shoveling more snow than they could handle.

"Hey, I got an idea!" said Benny excitedly, jumping up and down. "Let's burn the snow!"

"We can't do that, you idiot," said Lenny. "Besides, what would we do with all the ashes?"

The postal worker called in sick one day.

"I can't come in today to sort out the mail," he told his boss on the phone.

"What's wrong, have you lost your zip?"

A woman went to the zoo to apply for a job. When she arrived for the interview, the zookeeper told her he was looking for someone to dress up as a kangaroo to replace the real one that had been sent to another zoo.

"But I can't jump like a kangaroo," said the woman.

"Don't worry," the zookeeper reassured her. "We'll hide a trampoline behind some rocks and you can bounce up and down like the real thing."

The woman accepted and soon found herself in a kangaroo outfit leaping up and down on the trampoline. As the spectators cheered her, she got so caught up in the role that she bounced extra hard, then shot over the fence into the tiger's cage.

Scrambling to her feet, the woman began screaming hysterically, "Somebody help me! Help!"

The tiger inched closer and closer, then growled, "Shut up, lady, or we'll both lose our jobs!"

A coal miner hired three men to work for him.

"Okay," he instructed the first man. "Your job is to dig for the coal."

He turned to the second man, "Your job is to put the coal in the cart."

"What about me?" asked the third man.

"You take care of the supplies."

A few days later the miner returned to check up on them. The first man was digging for coal, the second was shoveling the coal into the cart, but the third man was nowhere in sight.

"Where's the other guy?" asked the miner. "He's supposed to be handling supplies."

Just then the third worker jumped out of the bushes, blowing a party whistler and shouting, "Surprise! Surprise!"

FLIP: My uncle lost his job as a bus driver, so he took up a life of crime.

FLOP: How did he do?

FLIP: He gave it up. Nobody would give him exact change.

A laboratory rat came home from work one night exhausted.

"How was it, honey?" asked his wife.

"It was very tiring," answered the rat. "I spent the entire day running through a maze with a bunch of other rodents."

"Oh, same old rat race, huh?" said his wife.

Determined that he was entitled to more money, Maurice walked into his boss's office and said, "Excuse me, sir, but I think I deserve a raise."

"I'm sorry, Maurice," replied his boss, "but you'll have to work yourself up first."

"I already have," said Maurice nervously. "Look— my hands are trembling."

The first day on the new job was a confusing one for Mr. Dithers. He stood in front of the office machine trying to figure out all the buttons.

"Need some help?" offered one of the secretaries.

"Yes, how does this thing work?" asked Mr. Dithers, brandishing a thick pile of papers in his hands.

The secretary took the papers from him and began to feed them into the machine. Mr. Dithers watched in fascination as the machine tore each sheet into shreds.

"Thank you so much," said Mr. Dithers when the last paper had been shredded. "Now where do the copies come out?"

TIP: What's the difference between a train engineer and a boxing referee?

TOP: One blows the whistle, the other whistles the blows.

SIGN AT A DRY CLEANER

> We'll clean for you.
> We'll press for you.
> We'll even dye for you.

JAN: What's an astronaut's favorite place on a computer?

VAN: The space bar.

Phil was on the top rung of a ladder, painting a house, while Bill stood on the ground, watching.

"Hey, up there!" Bill shouted suddenly to Phil. "Have you got a firm grip on that paintbrush?"

"I sure do," Phil replied.

"Hold on tight, then," said Bill. "I need to borrow the ladder for a minute."

Two hillbillies desperate for work went to the city to seek employment.

Spotting a sign with the words "TREE FELLERS WANTED," the first hillbilly remarked to the second, "Too bad there's only two of us or we could have gotten a job."

If astronauts are so smart, why are they always counting backwards?

An astronaut graduated near the bottom of his class. On his first mission into space, he was teamed up with an orangutan. The astronaut and the orangutan were each given an envelope that they were to open once they got into space.

Moments after blastoff, the orangutan opened his envelope, read the contents, and then began flicking buttons and hitting switches.

Excitedly opening his envelope, the astronaut was surprised to discover three words of instruction: "Feed the orangutan."

A man applied for a job at a construction firm.

"We take turns making coffee," said the supervisor. "Can you make coffee?"

"I sure can," said the man.

"Can you drive a forklift?"

"Why, how big is the coffee maker?"

DANA: What would you get if you crossed a banker with a kangaroo?
LANA: Vault-zing Matilda.

JESSE: What would you get if you crossed a germ with a comedian?
TESSIE: Sick jokes.

... SO THE DOCTOR SAYS, "WOULD YOU LIKE SYRUP ON YOUR PANCREAS?"

LEX: Sometimes it takes a thousand people to change one light bulb.
DEX: Why do you say that?
LEX: Because many hands make light work.

SON: Mom, did Dad leave for work without his glasses?
MOM: Yes, how did you guess?
SON: The garage door's missing.

KYLE: What's the difference between a baker and an overweight sleeper?

LYLE: One bakes the bread, the other breaks the bed.

The owner of a large factory decided to make a surprise visit and check up on his staff. Walking through the plant, he noticed a young man sitting lazily in the corner.

"Just how much are you being paid a week?" said the owner angrily.

"Three hundred bucks," replied the young man.

Taking out a fold of bills from his wallet, the owner slapped the money into the boy's hand and said, "Here's a week's pay. Now get out and don't come back."

Turning to one of the supervisors, he said, "How long has that lazy bum worked here, anyway?"

"He doesn't work here," said the supervisor. "He just came to deliver a pizza."

BOSS: If you can't keep up with the work, I'll have to get another clerk.
CLERK: Gosh, thanks, I could use some help.

SALESMAN: Guess what, I got two orders today!
BOSS: Congratulations! What were they?
SALESMAN: "Get out!" and "Stay out!"

The owner of a store was making the rounds when he spotted the new clerk.

"I trust your supervisor told you what you're supposed to be doing?" said the owner.

"You bet," said the clerk. "He told me to look real busy if I saw you coming my way."

Tourist to farmer:

"Excuse me, but do you have a pumpkin patch?"

"Why, do you have a leaky pumpkin?"

A construction worker accidentally dropped his trowel off the top of a building. The trowel fell ten stories and neatly sliced the ear off another worker.

As the man screamed in agony, the foreman quickly organized a search party to find the ear in the hope that the doctors could sew it back on again.

After a long search, someone cried out, "Here it is! I found the ear."

Taking one look at it, the injured worker sighed and said, "No, that can't be it. Mine had a pencil behind it."

15. Recess Riots

MOTHER: How was your first day at school?

TOMMY: Okay, but the teacher didn't give me a present.

MOTHER: Why would she give you a present?

TOMMY: Because she said, "Tom, sit there for the present."

DAD: Look at this report card! Your teacher says she can't teach you anything!

CHAD: I told you she was no good.

SCHOOL BULLY: If I hit you three times and said I'm sorry twice, what would you say?

SCHOOL DWEEB: I'd say you owe me an apology.

DAD: Why are you always at the bottom of your class?
BOBBY: What does it matter? They teach the same
thing at both ends.

Each day the son of the town baker brought his teacher a salted pretzel. One day she told him that although she appreciated the gesture, her doctor had advised her to cut down on salt.

"Don't worry," the boy reassured her. "I'll take care of it."

For the rest of the week boy brought his teacher pretzels with no salt on them.

"Tell your father the pretzels are very good," said the teacher one day. "I hope it's not a problem removing the salt?"

"No problem at all," said the boy, happily. "On the way to school I just lick it off!"

"All right, everybody on their backs with their feet up in the air!" the gym teacher shouted to his third-grade class. "I want you to pretend you're riding a bicycle."

Dropping to the floor, the students began rapidly kicking their legs in the sky—all except for one boy who slowly moved one foot in the air while the other leg lay limp on the floor.

"What's wrong with you?" asked the gym teacher.

"Isn't it obvious?" said the boy. "I've got a flat."

JASON: Hey, Dad, what would you say if I got a 100 on
my math test?
DAD: I'd be in such shock, I'd probably have a heart
attack.
JASON: I'm always looking out for your health, Dad.
That's why I settled for a 60.

THE KIDS IN MY SCHOOL
ARE SO RICH . . .

How rich are they?

They're so rich, they give their teachers an Apple and an IBM a day.

They're so rich, their treehouses have butlers.

They're so rich, their school has a mall in it.

They're so rich that for a science project, they bought a diamond mine.

Will, Phil and Gil were comparing report cards during recess.

"Guess what, I'm first in History!" exclaimed Will.

"And I'm first in Math," said Phil.

The others watched as Gil quickly tucked his report card back into his pocket and said, "Well, when the bell rings, I'm first out the door!"

Dana's father was trying to teach his son about self-confidence.

"You should avoid using negative words such as 'can't' and 'not,'" advised his father. "Do you think you can do that, son?"

"Well, Dad, I can't see why not."

LETTER TO MR. WIZARD

Dear Mr. Wizard:
How do fleas get from one place to another?
Signed, Buggy.

Dear Buggy:
They itch hike.

DAD: Would you mind explaining the meaning of this D and F on your report card?
SON: No problem, Dad. It stands for "Doing Fine."

DAD: I'm sorry you flunked your math test. How far were you from the right answer?
TAD: Three seats!

The human brain is a wonderful thing. It starts working the moment you get up in the morning and doesn't stop until the teacher calls on you.

While on a field trip to an amusement park, the teacher lost his wallet. Gathering the group together, he told the kids, "There was 300 dollars in my wallet. I will give a twenty dollar reward to anyone who finds it."
    A voice from the back of the group chimed in, "And I'll give $25!"

16. Tickle! Tickle!

A hungry man saw a sign in a restaurant window saying, "WE'LL PAY 100 DOLLARS TO ANYONE WHO ORDERS SOMETHING WE CAN'T MAKE."

When he was seated at his table he said to the waitress, "I'll have an elephant sandwich."

Digging into her apron, the waitress pulled out a roll of bills and handed the man a hundred dollars.

"What?" said the man as he pocketed the money, "no elephants today?"

"Oh, we have elephants, all right," sighed the waitress. "But we're all out of the big buns."

FLIP: What did one rug say to the other?
FLOP: "I'm mat about you."

A depressed man walked into a diner.

"What'll it be, buddy?" said the waitress.

"Chicken potpie and a kind word," replied the man.

When the waitress returned with the order the man asked, "Where's the kind word?"

"Don't eat the potpie," said the waitress.

PATIENT: I followed your advice for losing weight. I took off all my clothes and stood in front of a mirror.

DOCTOR: Did it work?

PATIENT: Well, yes—until they threw me out of the restaurant.

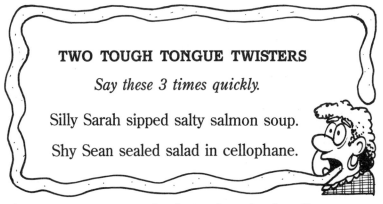

TWO TOUGH TONGUE TWISTERS

Say these 3 times quickly.

Silly Sarah sipped salty salmon soup.

Shy Sean sealed salad in cellophane.

A woman concerned about her husband's strange behavior went to a therapist.

"He thinks he's an opera star. He never stops singing," complained the woman. "What should I do?"

"Send him to me," suggested the therapist.

A week later the woman returned, delighted that her husband had made a complete recovery.

"Now he only sings once in a while," said the woman. "How did you do it?"

"It was simple," replied the therapist. "I just gave him a smaller part."

FOOD INSPECTOR: I'm afraid you have too many roaches in here.

RESTAURANT OWNER: How many am I allowed?

CUSTOMER: I just got out of prison and I'm dying for some home cooking.

WAITRESS: Hey, Al, bread and water in a dirty cup!

CUSTOMER: There's something wrong with this salad dressing.

WAITER: I can't understand it. We change the oil every six months.

CUSTOMER: Waiter, why do you have your finger on my hamburger?

WAITER: I don't want it to fall on the floor again.

CUSTOMER: I'm afraid I've had an accident with the salad.

WAITER: What happened?

CUSTOMER: My knife slipped and I cut the cockroach in half.

FIRST BOY: Hey, why is it taking you so long to make Kool-Aid?

SECOND BOY: You try getting two quarts of water in one of these tiny envelopes!

TEACHER: Henry, what are you doing with a hot dog on your ear?

HENRY: Uh-oh! I must have eaten my pencil.

TEACHER: Why do flamingoes stand on one leg?

CLASS CLOWN: If they didn't, they'd fall on their faces.

Three men stranded on a tropical island came upon a lamp buried in the sand. They rubbed the lamp and a genie appeared in a puff of smoke.

"I'll grant you three wishes," said the genie.

"I wish I was home with my family," said the first man. The genie waved his hand and POOF! The first man vanished in a puff of smoke.

"I wish I was back home with all my friends," said the second man and POOF! he too disappeared in a cloud of smoke.

The third man thought long and hard until the genie tapped his fingers impatiently and snapped, "What is it you wish?"

The third man sniffled and said: "I wish my two friends were back to keep me company."

An explorer in the Amazon was captured by a tribe of hostile natives. As they were about to torture him, he suddenly whipped out his pocket video game and pressed the ON button. The video game lit up, played music, and flashed a digital display, all to the delight of the natives, especially the chief of the tribe.

"Well, I guess I can go now," said the relieved explorer.

"Not so fast," said the chief. "You got any extra batteries?"

MOTHER: What's that odor I smell in the kitchen?
JUNIOR: I made a soup of vegetables and chewing
   tobacco.
MOTHER: What do you call it?
JUNIOR: Spit pea soup.

GREAT NEW COOKBOOKS

Fast Food Cookbook by Ivana Burger

No More Leftovers by M.T. Potts

Southern Cooking by Bob E. Kew

As he checked out of the Hillbilly Hotel, the man suddenly realized he had forgotten his luggage. Turning to the world's slowest bellhop, he shouted, "Run up to room 843 and see if I left my suitcase there."

"Sure thing," drawled the bellhop who started moving slowly towards the elevator.

"Hurry!" the man pleaded. "My plane leaves in ten minutes."

"Whatever you say," said the bellhop, then he disappeared.

Five minutes later the clerk returned, out of breath, and empty-handed.

"Well?" said the man desperately. "Did I leave my suitcase there?"

"Yep," replied the bellhop happily. "You left it on the bed."

SHILLY: Have you ever traced your ancestors?
SHALLY: Are you kidding, I can't draw worth a nickel.

BEST-SELLERS FROM THE NONFICTION SHELF

1. *The Sinking of the Titanic*
   by Mandy Lifeboat

2. *How to Make A's in School*
   by Hedda De Classe

3. *How to Raise the Dead*
   by Mort U. Aries

4. *Galloping Galaxies*
   by Saul R. System

5. *Home Dentistry*
   by I.M. Numb

6. *The Home Guide to Bullfighting*
   by Matt Adore

7. *Parachuting Made Easy*
   by Will E. Maykit

8. *How to Be a Happy Camper*
   by Lucinda Woods

9. *How to Recover from a Hospital Visit*
   by Gladys Over

10. *How to Paint Your Own Chapel*
    by Mike L. Angelo

WILMA: Hey, what kind of dial casts a shadow, but should never be asked the time?

VILMA: A crock-a-dial (crocodile).

DILLY: What's orange, good for your eyes, and jumps out of airplanes?

WILLY: Carrot-troopers.

KIT: What's the difference between Cinderella's shoe and a kid who plays hooky?

KAT: One's a glass slipper, the other's a class skipper.

JESS: Where does King Arthur keep his armies?

BESS: In his sleevies.

One of King Arthur's knights lost his way in the woods. As he wandered aimlessly in search of shelter, it began to rain and snow and the knight soon grew exhausted and hungry.

Coming upon a St. Bernard, the knight threw himself on the animal's back and the dog carried him to the nearest inn. Barely able to hold himself up, the knight managed to rap on the door.

When the innkeeper opened the door, the knight gasped, "Please—do you have a room available?"

"Sorry," said the innkeeper, "but we're all full."

The knight coughed and wheezed, "Then may I sit by your fire and warm myself?"

"Well, of course," replied the innkeeper as the St. Bernard dragged the man in. "I would never let a knight out on a dog like this."

Wise Man Says

A worm that falls asleep in King Arthur's apple will wake up in the middle of the knight.

Knock-knock!
Who's there?
Vanna.
Vanna who?
Vanna you gonna come out and play?

ARNIE: What's a frankfurter's favorite car?
MARNIE: A Rolls.

A man crossing a bridge encountered a small boy leaning over the railing, crying.

"What's the matter, son?" asked the man.

"My sandwich fell in the water," sobbed the boy.

"It must have a been a delicious sandwich," said the man. "Was it with cheese?"

"No!" cried the boy.

"Was it with bologna?"

"No!"

"What was it with then?"

"It was with my brother!"

Phil and Will went into a diner, took out their lunchboxes, and started eating their sandwiches.

"Hey!" said the waitress, "you can't eat your own sandwiches in here."

So Phil and Will swapped sandwiches.

DAFFY: What's the difference between a garbage truck and an army cafeteria?
LAFFY: One hauls a mess, the other's a mess hall.

ZIP: What's the difference between a gambler and a person who contributes to charities?
ZAP: One cashes in his chips, the other chips in his cash.

FIRST OCTOPUS: What do you hate most about being an octopus?
SECOND OCTOPUS: Washing my hands before dinner.

FRITZ: Sardines are the dumbest fish.
BLITZ: Why do you say that?
FRITZ: Who else would lock themselves in a can and leave the key outside?

Mother Computer scolding PC Junior:
"Wait till your data gets home!"

CUSTOMER: Waiter, there's a crack in this bowl.
WAITER: You ordered vegetable soup, didn't you?
CUSTOMER: Yes.
WAITER: Well, our vegetable soup has a leek in it.

SIGN AT ITALIAN RESTAURANT

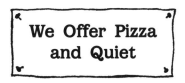

**We Offer Pizza
and Quiet**

CUSTOMER: Miss, I want to buy a pillowcase.
SALESGIRL: What size?
CUSTOMER: I'm not sure, but if it'll help, I wear a size
seven hat.

The groundskeeper at a park heard a splashing noise
in the pond and a voice crying out, "Help! Help!"

"Hey, can't you see the sign?" said the groundskeeper
to the man up to his neck in water. "It says 'No
Swimming.'"

"But I'm not swimming," gulped the man desperately,
"I'm drowning!"

"Oh, well, that's all right then."

"Mommy, mommy, the school is going to burn down!"
"How do you know?"
"Because we've been practicing for it all year."

JOE: My brother is connected to the police
department.
MOE: In what way is he connected?
JOE: By a pair of handcuffs.

NED: Knock, knock!
  TED: Who's there?
NED: Summons.
  TED: Summons who?
NED: Summons at the door.

GUSSY: Do fish perspire?
FUSSY: How do you think the sea gets so salty?

DAD: Son, this salad tastes funny. Did you wash it?
SON: Washed and waxed it, Dad.

WAITER: What can I get you, sir?
CUSTOMER: How about a nice lobster tail?
WAITER: Very well, sir. (*He takes out a book and reads*)
  "Once upon a time there was a little lobster..."

LOLLIE: Mother, why are lobsters red?
MOTHER: You would be, too, if you swam around in a
  supermarket tank with no clothes on.

17. Laughing It Up

I'VE BEEN GROWING THIS BEARD EVER SINCE I WAS A LITTLE SHAVER!

Once upon a time there was a family that was so cheap they called themselves the Cheapskates. The Cheapskates had three sons, Cheap, Cheaper, and Cheapest. One day Cheap decided to leave home and seek his future.

Twenty years later, Cheap returned to find his two brothers had beards growing all the way to the floor.

Bewildered, Cheap asked them, "Why is your hair so long?"

"It's all your fault," replied Cheapest. "You took the razor.

NIT: I put five dollars in the change machine.
WIT: What happened?
NIT: Would you believe it, I'm still me.

A little boy walked into a candy store with his arm curled up to his chest.

"Excuse me," said the clerk to the boy, "but did you injure your arm?"

"Oh, my gosh!" exclaimed the boy, "I lost my puppy."

Reassuring voice heard on the airplane intercom:

"Ladies and gentlemen, this is your captain speaking. I have good news and bad news. The bad news is that we have a hijacker on board. The good news is—he wants to go to Disneyworld!"

Did you hear about the moth that flew in to the two-year-old's birthday party? He burned his end at both candles.

DUSTIN: What did the pile of leaves say to the gardener?
JUSTIN: "Go ahead, rake my day."

FANNY: When my grandfather died he left us 500 clocks.

DANNY: I'll bet it'll take forever to wind up his estate.

NILLY: What would you get if you crossed a mouth with a tornado?

JILLY: A tongue twister!

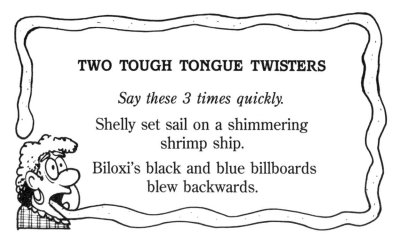

TWO TOUGH TONGUE TWISTERS

Say these 3 times quickly.

Shelly set sail on a shimmering shrimp ship.

Biloxi's black and blue billboards blew backwards.

KAREN: Last night I was visited by a woman with whiskers who granted me three wishes.

SHARON: Who might that be?

KAREN: My Hairy Godmother, of course.

Show me a magician's notebook and I'll show you a real spell binder.

WES: Knock-knock!

LES: Who's there?

WES: Hiya.

LES: Hiya who?

WES: Hiya someone to answer the door, will ya?

NON-FICTION BEST SELLER LIST

1. *I Was a Hell's Angel*
   by Hedda D. Pack

2. *The Magic of Fireworks*
   by Cis Boombah

3. *Autobiography of a Werewolf*
   by Harry S. Mann

4. *I Crossed the Atlantic*
   by Jethro Boat

5. *Astrology in Pictures*
   by Horace Cope

6. *Plane Building*
   by Upton Away

7. *Guide to Buying an Automobile*
   by Carlotta Munney

8. *Keeping Your Home Burglar Free*
   by Eudora S. Open

9. *The Facts about Suntan Lotion*
   by Justin Casey Burns

10. *The Zany Joke Book*
    by Y.B. Serious

MOTHER SNAKE: Why is Junior so bouncy?
FATHER SNAKE: You know very well he's viper-active.

SLIM: What goes "ring, ring" every morning at the wrong time?
JIM: A false alarm clock.

FIRST CAMPER: Knock-knock!
SECOND CAMPER: Who's there?
FIRST CAMPER: Charlotte.
SECOND CAMPER: Charlotte who?
FIRST CAMPER: Charlotte of mosquitoes around here.

GRACIE: What's the difference between a glacier and a snow cone?
TRACY: You can eat a snow cone in one afternoon.

SNIP: What vehicle doesn't burn gas, but is the most expensive to operate?
SNAP: A supermarket cart.

ZACK: My sister's on a raw fish diet.

JACK: Has she lost any weight?

ZACK: No, but she can balance a ball on her nose and bark like a seal.

On the day of his first parachute jump, Leonard listened carefully to the instructor's directions.

"Count to ten, then pull the first cord. If nothing happens, pull the second cord for the backup chute. When you land, a van will pick you up. Got it?"

"Got it," said Leonard and with that, he jumped from the plane, counted to ten, then pulled the cord. Nothing happened.

Quickly, he yanked the second cord. Still nothing.

As he fell to the ground, he mumbled angrily to himself, "I bet that darn van won't be there, either!"

Did you hear about the letter T having an identity crisis? It wants to be just like U.

TEX: Knock-knock!
DEX: Who's there?
TEX: Sanctuary.
DEX: Sanctuary who?
TEX: Sanctuary much!
DEX: You're welcome!

Mr. Dithers knew he was late when he spotted the ferry just a few feet from the dock. Running as fast as he could, he leaped across the water, barely landing on the boat's deck.

"That was sure close," said Mr. Dithers as a nearby stranger helped him to his feet.

"What's the hurry?" said the stranger. "This ferry's just arriving."

> Did you hear about the world's dumbest
> lottery? For the jackpot you win a dollar
> a year for a million years.

MARLA: Did you hear about the group of people who got stranded in the mall?
CARLA: They were shopwrecked.

DARREN: What famous nurse rarely got dressed in the morning?
KAREN: Florence Nightingown.

CINDY: I bet you five dollars I can spell "80" with just two letters.
MINDY: All right, you're on.
(Cindy writes the letters "A" and "T" on a piece of paper and collects the money.)

DOOFUS: How do you clear ice off the windows of tall buildings?

GOOFUS: With a sky scraper.

DORIS: What is lighter than a feather, but can't be held for five minutes?

MORRIS: Your breath.

It's a small world, but I wouldn't want to have to vacuum it.

CUSTOMER: Waiter, is this a fly in my soup?

WAITER: No, that's the chef. The last customer was a witch doctor.

TUTTI: What do mountain climbers' kids like to play?

FRUTTI: Height and Seek.

LANCE: What do you call a bird who tattles to the lifeguard?

VANCE: A pool pigeon.

HANK: What's the difference between a stool pigeon and an earthquake?

FRANK: One cracks under pressure, the other pressures under cracks.

He's so dumb he once got stuck on an escalator and didn't know how to get down.

NILES: Who gets all dressed up and draws on napkins?
MILES: Hanky Doodle Dandy.

CHUCKIE: What's worse than looking into the eye of a great white shark?
DUCKIE: Looking into his tonsils.

PERSONAL TRAINER: How do we know exercise keeps us healthy?
PERSONAL CLOWN: Did you ever see a germ on a rowing machine?

Knock-knock!
 Who's there?
Wilma.
 Wilma who?
Wilma lunch be ready soon?

A man hitchhiking in the mountains stopped at a monastery for a meal.

After finishing a platter of fish and chips, the man enjoyed it so much he went into the kitchen to compliment the chef.

"That was delicious," he said to one of the monks in an apron. "Are you the fish fryer?"

"No," he replied. "I'm the chip monk."

TIM: What kind of suit would you wear to a mermaid's wedding?

KIM: A wet suit, naturally.

DON: What's the difference between a Venice Street and painful dentistry?

RON: I haven't the faintest.

DON: One's a canal route, the other's a root canal.

JEN: Why did the clerk move the calendar away from the window?
BEN: Because it was a leap year.

FUZZY: What do you call a red-headed lady on a blue and white plane travelling from New York to London?
WUZZY: A passenger.

Once upon a time two giants named Andrea and Andy were playing tag when Andrea tripped Andy and he fell to the ground. The impact was so great it caused a crack in the earth a mile wide.

Their father ran out to see what happened.

"What is the meaning of this?" he cried.

"Don't look at me," said Andy. "It's not my fault, it's Andrea's fault."

Show me a post office on fire
and I'll show you a case of black mail.

HOLEY: I just read that somewhere there's a rabbit giving birth every second.
MOLEY: Gee whiz, somebody should find her and stop her!

POSTMAN: Is this letter for you? The name is blurry.
MAN: Couldn't be me. My name is Smith.

NELLY: What has three feet, three eyes and two bills?
KELLY: A duck with spare parts.

RIP: What would you get if you crossed a duck with a gator?
PIP: A quack-a-dile.

FREDDIE: Do you have holes in your underwear?
TEDDIE: I should say not!
FREDDIE: Then, how do you put them on?

Two caterpillars were sunning themselves on a leaf one day when a butterfly flew overhead.

Said the first to the second, "I'll tell you one thing— you'll never get me up in one of those things."

18. Party Har Har!

RUSS: What is grey, has a trunk but no tags, and keeps circling the airport?

GUS: An unclaimed elephant on the baggage carousel.

CHAD: What made nine passengers hurry off the Greyhound?

BRAD: A flea collar.

At a busy Italian restaurant a man asked the waitress if his order of spaghetti and meatballs would be long.

"Yes and no," replied the waitress.

"What do you mean yes and no?"

"Yes, the spaghetti will be long and no, the meatballs will be round."

After a long drive cross country a man stopped at a hotel for a rest. Extremely exhausted, he approached the clerk at the front desk and said, "Excuse me, sir. I'm tired, I've been driving all day, I have a headache, and my mind isn't working too well. Can you tell me what room I'm in?"

"Certainly," replied the clerk. "You're in the lobby."

RITA: What would you get if you crossed a canary with a carrier pigeon?
NITA: What do you get?
RITA: A singing telegram.

MARK: What would you get if you crossed a hot-air balloon with a ghost?
LARK: High spirits.

A group of five army recruits out on practice patrol got separated from the rest of the battalion. After a while they came to a bridge that had a sign saying, "CLEARANCE: 9 FEET." The five stopped, counted the number of feet among them and turned back.

SAL: What do you get when you cross a clock with a cigarette?
HAL: Second-hand smoke.

There was a football game between the elephants and the insects. Though the elephants got a good lead, the bugs soon came out fighting, eventually winning the game.

When it was over, the elephant coach shook hands with the insect coach and asked, "How did you manage to beat us?"

"In the second half," replied the insect, "we put in a centipede."

"But why didn't you use him in the first half?"

"Because he was too busy tying his shoelaces," said the insect coach.

Little Henry got a cello and played it night and day. Unfortunately, every time he plucked a string, the family dog would whine and howl to no end.

Unable to stand the dog's suffering any longer, one day Henry's baby sister stormed into his room and pleaded, "For goodness' sake! Why don't you play something the dog doesn't know!"

Did you hear about the mad inventor who created a knife that could slice four loaves of bread at one time? It was the world's first four-loaf cleaver.

A hillbilly on a trip around the world flew on a plane for the first time. Arriving in New York City, the plane made a neat landing and immediately a little red wagon drove up and refuelled the engine.

The next stop was London and as soon as the plane touched down, again a red wagon promptly rushed up to refuel. The same thing happened when they landed in Canada.

"These planes make wonderful time, don't they?" remarked a fellow passenger to the hillbilly.

"Sure do," said the hillbilly, "and that little red wagon ain't doin' too bad either!"

Refusing to surrender his money to a mugger, Mr. Cummings put up a fight. After a long struggle, the mugger finally overcame Mr. Cummings to discover only 57 cents in his pocket.

"You put up a fight like that for a lousy fifty-seven cents?" said the mugger.

"I'm sorry," said Mr. Cummings. "I thought you were after the 400 dollars I hid in my shoe."

Did you hear about the lion that swallowed a computer? Talk about a mane frame!

MOLLY: We're having a romantic dish for dinner tonight.
JOLLY: Oh, no, not mush, again.

HE: Please whisper those three little words that'll have me dancing on air.
SHE: Go hang yourself.

Silly Sam had never cooked a day in his life, but decided to surprise his wife on her birthday. He went to the barn, selected a chicken, plucked it, then popped it in the oven.

An hour later he realized he hadn't turned the oven on. As he pulled open the door, the chicken sat up and said, "Look, mister, either turn on the heat or give me back my feathers!"

A woman complained to her psychiatrist about her scientist husband. "I'm afraid he spends more time with bacteria than he does with me," said the wife.

"Oh, don't bacilli," replied the doctor.

WIFE: Doctor, our marriage has never been the same ever since my husband started thinking he was a human boomerang.

DOCTOR: Don't worry, he'll come around.

MOTHER: Why are all your boyfriends named William?

SALLY: Because I'm a bill collector.

LITTLE BROTHER: I'm tougher than Tarzan.

OLDER BROTHER: What makes you tougher?

LITTLE BROTHER: I can beat my chest without screaming.

Passing by a floral shop, a man spied a sign that said, "Say It With Flowers."

Stepping inside, he said to the clerk, "I'd like a flower, please."

"Just one flower?"

"Yes," he replied. "I'm a man of few words."

SPACE ALIEN (*to girlfriend*): "Do you want to try that new restaurant on the moon?"

"I hear the food is good, but there's no atmosphere."

LEM: My girlfriend is so smart she has brains enough for two!

CLEM: Sounds like the right girl for you.

DIT: My new boyfriend lights up every time he sees me.

DOT: Sounds like a perfect match.

Did you hear about the groom who tried to kiss his bride in the fog and mist (missed)?

BILL: You owe me a dollar for that bottle of honey.

JILL: What honey?

BILL: Gosh, I didn't know you cared.

As Goofy George had a habit of giving his wife strange Christmas gifts, she was not surprised when he came one night carrying a tiny, branchless tree. Attached to a lone limb was a shotgun shell.

"All right, George," said his wife, truly stumped this time. "What is it?"

"Why, honey," George smiled, "it's a cartridge in a bare tree."

FIRST MAN: I think my wife wants to get rid of me.
SECOND MAN: Why do you say that?
FIRST MAN: She keeps handing me my electric razor.
SECOND MAN: What's wrong with that?
FIRST MAN: While I'm taking a bath?

BEN: When I grow up I'm going to marry the girl next door.
LEN: Why the one next door?
BEN: Because I'm not allowed to cross the street.

POLICE OFFICER: So you say a strange man grabbed you and kissed you? What did he look like?
WOMAN VICTIM: I don't know. I always keep my eyes closed when I'm being kissed.

What am I?
I never move. I have no feet, but I wear shoes. What am I?
The sidewalk.

SHE: Lonnie has it first. Phil has it last. Girls have it once. Boys never have it.

HE: I give up.

SHE: The letter "l."

FLOSSY: How do you stop an elephant from slipping through the eye of a needle?

MOSSY: How?

FLOSSY: Tie a knot in his tail.

IGGY: Why doesn't the Board of Health let bakeries sell orange juice?

ZIGGY: Because bakers can't be juicers.

One night Fred walked into the bowling alley to play his weekly Tuesday night game. As he was tying his shoes, one of the balls shot up from the chute and knocked him unconscious, causing severe amnesia.

After disappearing for ten years, one day Fred miraculously returned, his memory back. His wife tearfully embraced him and then dashed to the phone and started dialing.

"Who are you calling?" said Fred.

"Everybody," exclaimed his wife. "We're going to have a big party to celebrate your return."

"No way," said Fred. "Not on my bowling night."

"What's more accurate than a digital watch and able to tell time with a single bound?"

"Clock Kent."

GIGGLY GREETING CARDS

To circus seals—BEST FISHES!

To sick lemons—
       HOPE YOU'RE FEELING BITTER!

To sick skunks—GET SMELL SOON!

To vacationing rabbits—BUNNY VOYAGE!

To lonely snakes—I HISS YOU!

To married bugs—HAPPY ANT-IVERSARY!

To maple trees—SAPPY BIRTHDAY!

To ghosts on the first of the year—
       HAPPY BOO YEAR!

19. Immortal Chortles

A farmer went to a fair. He jumped for joy when he saw they had old-fashioned airplane rides. The problem was he didn't want to pay $25 dollars for one ride.

"Tell you what I'll do," said the pilot. "If you can fly with me and not say a single word, I'll give you every cent in my pocket. Otherwise, you pay full price." The farmer agreed and before long they were up in the sky, flying upside down, and weaving through the clouds in every direction.

When they landed the pilot shook the farmer's hand in amazement, "You didn't speak a single word. How did you do it?"

"It was sure tough," replied the farmer. "Especially, when your wallet slipped out of your pocket."

While their parents were hosting a party, little Bobby and his sister took off their clothes and began to walk around the dinner table. Too embarrassed to say anything, their parents acted as if nothing was happening and the guests, out of courtesy, did the same.

Later, when they had returned to their room, Bobby remarked to his sister, "See, I told you it was vanishing cream!"

ROONY: What's the difference between a clumsy acrobat on ice and a gutsy acrobat at Niagara Falls?
CLUNY: One falls over the barrels, the other barrels over the falls.

A group of master chess players gathered in a New England hotel lobby for the annual HOLIDAY CHESS CONVENTION. As each player tried to better the other with stories of great moves and matches, the bragging got out of hand and soon turned to shouting.

"That's enough!" shouted the hotel manager, who couldn't take the noise any longer. "If there's one thing I can't stand, it's chess nuts boasting in an open foyer."

STU: What side of a killer shark should you stay away from?

LOU: The inside.

JENNY: Knock-knock!

LENNY: Who's there?

JENNY: Tumor.

LENNY: Tumor who?

JENNY: Tumor weeks to summer vacation!

Did you hear about the new cologne for weaklings? It smells like the school bully.

A man went into a greasy diner, ordered a milkshake, and then realized he had to go the bathroom. Worried someone might steal his drink, he took a paper napkin and wrote on it "World's Strongest Weight Lifter." Leaving the warning under the glass, he disappeared into the men's room.

When he returned a few minutes later, the glass was empty and under it was a new napkin with a message that said, "World's Fastest Runner."

Mr. Winterbottom arrived at the airport and spotted a computerized weighing machine in the lobby. Curious, he dropped a quarter in the slot and stepped on it as a voice announced, "You are five feet, ten inches tall, weigh 165 pounds, and you are taking a plane to Australia."

Impressed by the machine's accuracy, he tried it again. "You are five feet, ten inches tall," the voice repeated, "weigh 165 pounds, and you are taking a plane to Australia."

The third time he decided to try to fool the machine. He took his suitcase into the men's room and changed into a different coat and tie. Pulling his hat over his ears to hide his face, Winterbottom dropped another quarter into the machine. "You are five feet, ten inches tall, weigh 165 pounds," the voice announced, then added, "and while you were changing your clothes, you missed the plane to Australia."

SIGN ON NUCLEAR POWER PLANT DOOR

Gone Fission.

Mr. Witherby was cleaning out his attic and found an old claim ticket for a pair of shoes he had sent to be repaired nearly ten years earlier. Figuring he had nothing to lose, he went to the shoe repair shop and presented the ticket to the repair man. A few minutes later the man reappeared, looking very optimistic.

"Well, did you find them?" asked Mr. Witherby.

"Yes," replied the man. "They'll be ready next Tuesday."

On Halloween three boys went to a Star Trek costume party. The first boy walked through the door wearing pointed ears and arched eyebrows. The host of the party looked at him and said, "What have you come as?"

"Isn't it logical?" replied the boy. "I'm Mr. Spock."

The second boy entered wearing black boots, black pants, and a red jumper.

"And what have you come as?" said the host.

"Aye, can't you see?" replied the second boy. "I'm Scotty, the engineer."

Finally, the third boy stepped forward dressed in the shape of a tree.

The host looked baffled and asked, "And what are you?"

"Isn't it obvious?" snapped the boy. "I'm the Captain's log?"

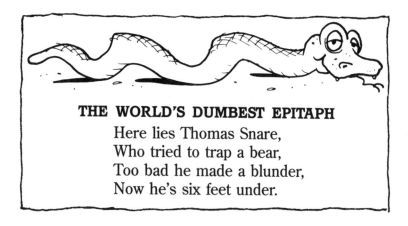

THE WORLD'S DUMBEST EPITAPH
Here lies Thomas Snare,
Who tried to trap a bear,
Too bad he made a blunder,
Now he's six feet under.

A man called a hotel to make a room reservation.

"Do you have rooms with a shower and bath?"

"Sure do," replied the clerk.

"What's the difference?"

"Well, in a shower you stand up."

Dexter came home from school with a black eye and a bloody nose. While his father patched him up, he asked, "What happened to you, Dexter?"

"I challenged Billy to a fight," said Dexter. "But I told him he could have his choice of weapons."

"Well, that seems fair."

"Yes, but I never thought he'd choose his sister."

As the storm began to rage, the absent-minded professor started outside when his wife stopped him, asking, "Where do you think you're going?"

"I'm going out to water the flowers," replied the professor.

"But it's raining outside!" said his wife.

"You're right," said the professor, closing the door and walking to the closet. "I'd better take my umbrella."

DOCTOR: Take one of these pills once a day for the rest of your life.

PATIENT: But there's only seven pills in this bottle.

DOCTOR: I know.

Sam went into a drug store and bought a box of mothballs. The next day he returned and purchased a second box. When he came back the third day, the clerk's curiosity got the best of him and he said, "You sure must have a lot of moths in your house!"

"I do," said Sam. "And I can't take it anymore. I've been throwing these balls at them for two days and I haven't hit a single one!"

...THIS GUY IS STARTING TO BUG US!!!...

KERI: Wouldn't it be neat to know the time and place that you were going to die?

TERI: What good would that do you?

KERI: I wouldn't show up.

It was Mr. Hardy's lifelong dream to go scuba diving, and one day he decided to do it. He went to a sporting goods store and spent a fortune on scuba diving gear. He got everything he needed and more—outfit, oxygen tanks—the works.

The next morning he drove out to a reef, put on his gear, and plunged into the ocean. As he dove deeper, he spotted a man swimming near the bottom in just his swimming trunks. Getting out his underwater notepad, Mr. Hardy scrawled a message to the man that said, "How can you swim without scuba-diving gear?"

The man took the notepad from Mr. Hardy and wrote back, "I'm not swimming, you idiot! I'm drowning!"

Benjamin was on safari deep in the Amazon jungle when he found himself surrounded by fierce-looking natives.

As they moved closer, Harold suddenly remembered an old trick he saw in a movie. Quickly, he pulled out his lighter and flicked the flame towards the leader of the natives.

Astonished, the leader jumped back and gasped, "That's incredible!"

"You better believe it's incredible," said Benjamin, waving the fire at him.

"It certainly is," said the leader. "I can't remember the last time I saw a lighter that worked the first time you flicked it."

LOU: What is the difference between a person who lives in Australia and a person who sleeps under a feather quilt?
STU: One's down under, the other's under down.

Rodney, an unsuccessful ventriloquist, gave up his act and became a spiritual medium. One day a woman whose husband had recently died came to consult him.

"Can you make my dead husband talk to me again?" she asked.

"Lady, not only can I make him talk," replied Rodney, "but I can do it while drinking a glass of water."

SNIP: Why did the fly head for the alarm clock?
SNAP: He wanted to land on time.

The absent-minded professor's life changed dramatically when he got a brand-new hearing aid. Showing if off to his wife, he said, "This is the best hearing aid in the world. In fact, I haven't heard this well since I was kid."

"What kind is it, anyway?" asked his wife.

The professor looked at his watch and replied, "Oh, it's about ten minutes to five."

The man pulled his car to the side of the road when he heard the police siren.

"How long have you been riding around without a taillight?" asked the officer.

"Oh, no!" screamed the man, jumping out and dashing to the rear of the car.

"Calm down," said the officer. "It isn't that serious."

"Wait'll my family finds out."

"Where's your family?"

"They're in the trailer that was hitched to the car!"

One morning Stu and Lou went fishing. Before long Lou had caught twenty fish while Stu caught nothing. The next day they went back and again Lou snagged more fish than he could handle while Stu was left empty-handed.

On the third day Stu decided to fish by himself. He got up early and snuck out to the river. Dropping his line into the water, immediately he felt a tug. When he yanked it up, there was a note attached to it that said, "Where's Lou?"

NIT: This year I took French, Spanish and Algebra.
WIT: Great, let's hear you say "goodbye" in Algebra.

ABOUT THE AUTHORS

Philip Yates and Matt Rissinger, also the authors of *Great Book of Zany Jokes,* used to be two very serious guys. As legend has it, one day while waiting for a bus they spotted a shiny coin on the sidewalk. Knowing that a penny saved is a penny earned, they both swooped for it at the same instant, clunking heads and cracking their funny bones. In short, they were both knocked silly.

Seriously, Matt and Phil spend most of their spare time writing jokes. They work out by performing jumping jokes, chuckle-ups, and long-distance punning at schools and libraries all over the East Coast. Matt lives near Valley Forge, Pennsylvania, with his wife, Maggie, and two daughters, Rebecca and Emily. Philip lives in Prospect Park, Pennsylvania, with his cat, Sam, and plans to marry Maria Beach in the near future.

Oh, and about that penny. They didn't spend it. They invested it. When you write silly jokes for a living, you never have enough cents.

INDEX